Donburi
Mania

By Kentaro Kobayashi
Photography by Hideo Sawai

VERTICAL.

Contents
Numbers in parentheses indicate recipe page

Note: In this book 1 cup = 200 ml, 1 tablespoon = 15 ml, 1 teaspoon = 5 ml.

Chart Topping

I love Donburi. All of them.
Sure, my preferences change with my mood and even with the weather,
but there are the special few on my permanent list of favorites
that I find eternally and exceptionally irresistible.
I could eat them anytime, anywhere, and in any amount.
I present to you the best of Kentaro's Donburi recipes.

Donburi

Top the rice, and you're on top of the world. That's the "Donburi Spirit."

The minute you top a bowl of steaming hot rice with something delicious, what was once just rice and a simple side dish becomes a donburi. It may sound like a simple change, but try it and you'll see. On top or on the side, that's what makes all the difference.

With the exception of dishes that just don't go with hot rice, any recipe is fair game. It's sure to be delicious. Combining the two is all "pros" and no "cons." Even steak, served on top of rice, becomes a great one-dish feast. If it were all by itself, the flavorful meat juices would go to waste. But as a donburi, they are absorbed into the rice, making the grains all the more tasty. That's one of the things that make donburi truly *un-toppable*.

Pork Steak Donburi
Enjoy high-class flavor without the cutlery confusion

Cook a pork steak nice and brown, spread it over rice, and you have a feast in a bowl. Just thinking about that rice steeped in pork juice will get your stomach rumbling.

Use high heat to coat with sauce quickly

Ingredients (Serves 2)
2 pork shoulder steaks (5 to 7 oz (150 to 200 g) each)
1/2 each red, yellow and green bell peppers
1 bunching onion (or sub. green onion or leek)
A: Dash each grated ginger and grated garlic
   2 Tbsp water
   1 tsp soy sauce
   1 Tbsp each miso, sake (or cooking wine), mirin (sweet cooking wine), and sugar
2 Tbsp vegetable oil
Salt and pepper, to taste
2 servings steaming hot rice
Roasted white sesame seeds, to taste

Instructions
1) Remove stems and seeds of bell peppers and cut lengthwise into 6 to 8 equal sized pieces. Slice bunching onion into appx. 3" (7 to 8 cm) segments.
2) Make several cuts on both sides of pork loin. Combine mixture A.
3) Heat frying pan and add 1 Tbsp of oil. Add bell peppers and sprinkle on salt. Stir-fry at high heat until peppers are lightly browned and tender and remove from pan.
4) Lightly wipe off pan and return to heat. Add 1 Tbsp oil and place pork in pan. Sprinkle with salt and pepper, cover with lid and cook at medium heat. Cook until well browned and flip. Place onions around meat. Cook at medium heat, occasionally turning onions over.
5) When meat is thoroughly cooked and browned on both sides and onions are charred, add mixture A and coat well.
6) Let pork rest on a plate for a few minutes to retain juiciness. Slice pork thinly. Arrange on top of rice in bowls along with cooked peppers and scallions. Sprinkle with roasted sesame seeds.

Can't get enough rice? That's the sign of a properly prepared Donburi.

It's the rice that makes the donburi.
Sure, the stuff on top takes a lot more time and preparation, but all of that, really, is meant to enhance the rice. It just serves to make the rice more delectable.
Marinate some chicken, coat it with starch, fry it 'til it's crispy and toss it on top of a bowl of rice. This whole process is all to bring out the sweetness of the rice. In some cases you have extra cooking juices.
Sometimes the flavor is stronger than usual. And sometimes, like with Japanese-Style Fried Chicken, you just fry some chicken and place it on rice. Various methods, but all with one purpose: to whet your appetite for rice.
The rice is the main ingredient. Don't forget!

Japanese-Style Fried Chicken Donburi
No sauce needed to keep the rice rolling in

Japanese-Style Fried Chicken is well seasoned, so no sauce is needed. Fresh, crisp lettuce helps to link the flavors of crunchy fried chicken and steaming hot rice.

Coat with cornstarch carefully

Ingredients (Serves 2)
2 large chicken thighs (12 to 14 oz (350 to 400 g) total)
A: Dash each grated ginger and grated garlic
   1 1/2 Tbsp soy sauce
   1 tsp each sake (or cooking wine) and sesame oil
   1/2 tsp sugar
   1/2 tsp salt
Oil for deep frying (The best temperature for frying is 350° to 375°)
Potato (or corn) starch
2 servings steaming hot rice
2 large leaves lettuce, roughly shredded
Mayonnaise, to taste (appx. 1 Tbsp)
Seven-spice powder (or sub. cayenne pepper)

Instructions
1) Remove fat from chicken and cut into large bite-size pieces. Combine mixture A ingredients in a bowl, add chicken, and massage seasonings in well by hand.
2) Fill a pan with oil 1 1/4" (3 cm) deep and heat to medium high. Place starch in a separate bowl and coat chicken evenly. Grip the coated chicken firmly to ensure the starch sticks well.
3) Place chicken in oil, skin side down. Use medium high heat and do not touch chicken until edges become crispy. Then, fry until golden brown, occasionally turning chicken over. Once browned, raise heat to high and stir oil with a sweeping motion before removing for a crispy finish.
4) Serve rice in bowls and top with fried chicken and lettuce. On the side add mayonnaise sprinkled with seven-spice powder, if desired.

Note
Poke the thickest part of the meat with a skewer. If the juice that runs out is clear, it's cooked through.

Eat when you're hungry. Hunger is the best spice.

Steaming hot rice with a sunny-side up egg on top. That's the Sunny-Side Donburi. You're probably thinking, "That's it?" Yup, that's it. That's all there is to it. Donburi, if you ask me, shouldn't require fancy tricks or special ingredients. You don't have to put in lots of time and trouble, or concentrate too hard on methods and materials. If you're hungry, whip it up and gobble it down just like that.
That's what donburi are all about.
That's how it is with the Sunny-Side Donburi. Open the fridge. Got eggs? Got ham? Then you're ready to go.
Cook the eggs just right so the yolk is good and gooey, pour over rice, then sprinkle on soy sauce. Simple, but so delicious, more time-consuming fancy cuisine can't compete.

Sunny-Side Donburi
This surprisingly tasty donburi is top-ranked by fans

This donburi has many, many fans. They say I opened their eyes to the true purpose of the sunny-side up egg. I top it off with freshly ground black pepper.

Doubly delicious with ham and black pepper

Ingredients (Serves 1)
2 slices ham
2 eggs
1 tsp vegetable oil
Salt and pepper, to taste
1 serving steaming hot rice
Soy sauce, to taste

Instructions
1) Heat pan and add oil. Arrange ham in pan and break eggs over the ham. Sprinkle with salt and pepper. Cover and cook on low heat until a thin film forms on the surface of the yolks.
2) Serve rice in a bowl and slide egg and ham on top. Add soy sauce and pepper to taste.

Note
If you have a large enough pan, you can cook 2 or 3 portions at once. Just split the eggs with a spatula and slide on top of separate rice bowls. Don't worry if it looks a little messy.

In the world of Donburi, the egg is a hero.

I take my hat off to the egg.
Eggs are indispensable when making donburi.
The reason is simple: without eggs, you can't make simmered egg sauce. And donburi without egg sauce is simply unthinkable!
Therefore, I take my hat off to the egg.
Let the egg trickle over the fork as you pour it in a sweeping circle. Cover with a lid immediately and simmer briefly.
Turn off heat and let it steam. Easy enough, but there is more to it than meets the eye.
You have to simmer the egg sauce just right so it's not too soupy or too cooked.
It's the light, fluffy, creamy texture that makes simmered egg sauce so delicious.
I mention cooking time for reference in the recipes, but try experimenting to find what works best for you.

Deluxe Pork Cutlet Donburi

1 fried pork cutlet + 2 eggs = a feast for the eyes and stomach!

This is a staple in the world of donburi. Buy a pork cutlet premade, or make your own from scratch. Either way, this is a tasty treat.

The key to success is cooking the egg just right

Ingredients (Serves 1)

1 store-bought pork cutlet (Or make your own: using a thin boneless chop, season with salt and pepper, dredge in about 1 Tbsp. flour, coat with 1 lightly beaten egg, and dip into Panko bread crumbs. Fry in oil until golden brown.)
1/2 small onion
2 to 3 *mitsuba* leaves (or sub. watercress or chervil)
2 eggs
1/2 C (100 ml) diluted Japanese noodle sauce (see reference guide)
1 to 1 1/2 tsp sugar
1 serving steaming hot rice

Instructions

1) Toast pork cutlet in a toaster oven until crispy and cut into bite size pieces. (If making your own, fry until golden, let rest on plate, then cut into pieces.) Slice onion thinly along the grain. Remove root end of *mitsuba* (or watercress) leaves and cut to a length of 2" (5 cm). Lightly beat 1 egg just enough to mix yolk and white.

2) Bring noodle sauce and sugar to boil in a small pan. Add sliced onion and simmer on medium heat until tender and translucent. Reduce heat to low and lay pork cutlet pieces in pan. Add egg, trickling over chopsticks or fork, pouring in a circular motion. Sprinkle in *mitsuba* (or watercress) leaves.

3) Crack other egg over cutlet and immediately cover. Simmer on low heat for 30 to 40 seconds and check if egg white has congealed; if not, continue cooking. Turn off heat once egg white is cooked and leave covered for another 20 seconds to steam.

4) Serve over rice in bowl.

Note

For a hearty, freshly fried flavor, toast the store-bought fried pork cutlet until the breading is hot and crispy.

Donburi is the ultimate one-plate dish.

With donburi, the rice and side dish are served together in one bowl as a complete meal. Or I should say that the minute you make donburi you've made a complete meal. That's what's so great about donburi. Even an ordinary serving of stir-fried veggies can be transformed into an impressive Stir-fried Veggie Medley Donburi.

Just rice and vegetable stir-fry would make for a pretty lonely dinner table. But make it into a donburi and you have yourself a festive and fun meal. And you get good nutritional balance in the bargain, too, with vegetables, protein, and carbohydrates all in one bowl. When rice and stir-fry seem like too *little* to stomach, don't hesitate to transform the two into a donburi. Donburi are truly revolutionary.

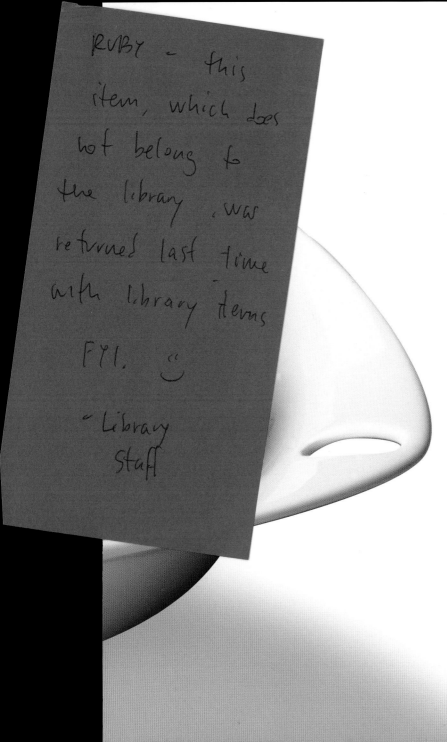
Stir-fried Veggie Medley Donburi

Rice steeped in sautéed vegetable juices— yum!

It is as easy as topping rice with a vegetable stir-fry. But take a bite and you'll realize the advantage of turning it into a donburi. As a side dish, the juices from the sautéed veggies are left wasted on the plate. But as a donburi, they can be thoroughly enjoyed as they soak into the rice. Aren't donburi just marvelous?

Fried tofu and shrimp add a full and robust flavor

Ingredients (Serves 2)

5 1/4 oz (150 g) pork shoulder meat, thinly sliced
1/2 sheet thin fried tofu (or sub. Tofu Cutlet)
1/8 head cabbage
2" (5 cm) carrot stick, peeled
1 clove garlic, 1 nub ginger
1 Tbsp sesame oil
1/2 C bean sprouts
2 to 3 Tbsp *sakura* (dwarf) shrimp (or salad shrimp)
1 Tbsp sake (or cooking wine)
1 tsp soy sauce
Pinch sugar
Salt and pepper, to taste
2 servings steaming hot rice

Instructions

1) Cut cabbage and pork into large bite-size pieces. Cut carrot in half, then into 1/7" (3 mm) half-moon slices. Cut fried tofu into 1/5" (5 mm) strips. Mince garlic and ginger.
2) Add sesame oil, garlic, and ginger to a heated pan. Sauté on low heat until fragrant. Add pork and sprinkle with salt and pepper. Raise heat to high and stir-fry.
3) When meat is lightly browned, add carrot, fried tofu, bean sprouts, cabbage, and shrimp in that order and stir-fry just until vegetables are tender. Add sake (or cooking wine) and stir-fry briskly. Add soy sauce and sugar and mix well. Add additional salt and pepper to taste.
4) Serve rice in bowls and top with stir-fried vegetables. Sprinkle with pepper.

Donburi magic has a certain trick to it.

Sometimes you have more simmering liquid than usual when cooking, and sometimes you have less. Sometimes the flavor is a little stronger or weaker. Maybe you cut the ingredients smaller. Or do the opposite, and slap the whole portion uncut onto the rice. Simple little things, but they can make a big difference.

The usual marinade for sardines has a strong vinegar flavor, but with donburi the marinade is absorbed into the rice, so it shouldn't be too strong. Serve the fish whole, perched delectably on top of the rice. Little things like that add up to make this a scrumptious feast. Of course, there are cases where all you need to do is slide the topping onto the rice. Sometimes you need to pull a few tricks out of your hat to make the donburi magic work.

Grilled Marinated Sardine Donburi

Enjoy a nice blend of Chinese and Japanese flavors

Sardines are cheap, nutritious and yummy. They're easy to cook with, too, even for people not fond of cooking fish. Grill them, marinate them, then smack them on top of rice.

Add an accent of fragrant *shiso* leaves!

Ingredients (Serves 2)
4 small sardines
1/2 onion
10 *shiso* leaves (or sub. basil or mint leaves)
1/2 nub ginger
2 red chili peppers
A: 1 Tbsp soy sauce
　 1 Tbsp mirin (sweet cooking wine)
　 1 Tbsp sesame oil
　 1 tsp oyster sauce
2 servings steaming hot rice
Roasted white sesame seeds, to taste

Instructions

1) Slice open undersides of sardines and remove innards. Remove heads if desired. Wash well under running water and pat dry. Grill until crispy.
2) While grilling, thinly slice onion lengthwise and soak in water for 5 minutes. Julienne ginger and shiso (or basil) leaves. Remove stems and seeds of chili peppers. Place ingredients in a shallow dish, add mixture A and stir.
3) Place grilled fish in dish and coat with marinade. Marinate for 5 minutes.
4) Serve rice in bowls and top with grilled marinated sardines. Sprinkle with roasted sesame seeds.

Voluminous donburi that keep the rice rolling in.
Donburi that satisfy even the biggest appetite. That's what this chapter is all about.
You don't need to make anything fancy. All you need is a bowl of rice generously topped with
its perfect match, and you have a superb, super-sized donburi.

"Super Size" Donburi

Ginger Roasted Pork Donburi

Munch away at plentiful, crispy cooked meat atop a fresh, crunchy bed of thinly sliced cabbage. Serve with Potato Salad and Red Miso Soup.

Recipe on page 20

Stewed Pork Donburi

Coated in plenty of flavorful sauce
for lip-smacking goodness
Serve with Salted *Komatsuna*

Recipe on page 20

Melty Cheesy
Meat Sauce Donburi

Thick, rich and irresistible

Recipe on page 21

Pork Stroganoff Donburi

**Rich and mellow,
a perfect match for rice**

Recipe on page 21

Ginger Roasted Pork Donburi

The rich flavor of oyster sauce is the key

Photo on page 16

I always use thinly sliced meat when making ginger roasted pork, especially for donburi. Wrap a bite of rice and crispy cabbage in a slice of pork coated in rich sauce, and before you know it the whole bowl will have disappeared.

Ingredients (Serves 2)
7 oz (200 g) thinly sliced pork shoulder meat
A: 1/2 nub ginger, grated
   2 Tbsp water
   1 Tbsp each sake, soy sauce, and mirin (sweet cooking wine)
   1 tsp each oyster sauce and sesame oil
1 Tbsp vegetable oil
Dash of salt and pepper
2 servings steaming hot rice
Cabbage, shredded
Mayonnaise, to taste

Instructions
1) Combine mixture A.
2) Add oil to a heated pan. Place pork in pan and sprinkle with salt and pepper. Cook on high heat.
3) Turn over meat when browned. Once both sides are cooked, pour in mixture A and coat meat.
4) Serve rice in bowls and top with cabbage and pork. Add mayonnaise on the side.

Note
Some people cook ginger roasted pork after allowing the meat to soak in the sauce, but I recommend adding the sauce while cooking. It's easier to keep the meat from burning, and it comes out more tender.

Potato Salad recipe on page 88
Red Miso Soup recipe on page 95

Stewed Pork Donburi

Allow the flavors to absorb as the meat stews

Photo on page 17

Rice steeped in sweet and spicy sauce, stewed pork so tender it melts in your mouth, boiled egg drowning in sauce. Take alternate bites of each and you have a one-way ticket to culinary heaven.

Ingredients (Serves 2)
10 1/2 oz (300 g) pork belly
Appx. 5 C water
Dash salt
1 nub ginger
A: 2 1/2 Tbsp sugar
   2 Tbsp each soy sauce, mirin (sweet cooking wine), sake (or cooking wine), water
2 boiled eggs, shelled
2 servings steaming hot rice
Chopped spring onions (or scallions), to taste
Roasted white sesame seeds, to taste
Japanese mustard (or hot mustard), to taste

Instructions
1) Cut pork belly into 4/5" (2 cm) cubes. Thinly slice ginger. Bring water to boil in a large pot, add a dash of salt, pork, and ginger. Bring to boil again, then turn heat to low. Simmer, occasionally removing foam that floats to the surface, for 1 to 2 hours until meat is tender enough that a skewer or fork can be easily inserted.
2) Remove from heat and let cool. Once cooled, remove clumps of fat floating on the surface. Set aside meat and 1 cup (200 ml) simmering stock.
3) Get a new pan and add mixture A and 1 cup of simmering stock and heat until sugar melts. Add pork and cover, leaving lid slightly askew. Simmer for 20 minutes on low heat, occasionally pouring stock over meat. Add boiled eggs and simmer for another 10 minutes. Add water as needed while simmering.
4) Serve rice in bowls and top with simmered pork and sauce. Top with spring onions (or scallions) and roasted sesame seeds and add mustard on the side, if desired.

Salted *Komatsuna* recipe on page 85

Melty Cheesy Meat Sauce Donburi

Marbled cheesy sauce makes for a mouthful of joy

Photo on page 18

Hot melted cheese winds its way through the rice, and the next minute tangy meat sauce captures your taste buds. This is a must-try donburi.

Ingredients (Serves 2)

7 oz (200 g) ground beef
1 pack mushrooms (appx. 2 1/2 oz)
1 bunch spinach
1 Tbsp olive oil
2 cloves garlic, minced
1 Tbsp white wine
4 Tbsp shredded mozzarella cheese
1 small can whole tomatoes
1 Tbsp flour
1 tsp oregano
1/2 to 1 tsp nutmeg
Salt and pepper, to taste
2 servings steaming hot rice

Instructions

1) Cut mushrooms lengthwise into 3 to 4 parts. Boil spinach in water with a dash of salt, then "shock" spinach in ice water to stop cooking and set color. Drain well and squeeze out excess water, then cut to 2" (5 cm) lengths.
2) In a pan, sauté garlic in olive oil on low heat until fragrant. Add ground beef and sauté on high heat while breaking up beef with a spatula.
3) When beef turns brown, add mushrooms and sauté until mushrooms are coated with oil. Add white wine and sauté. Add flour, oregano, and nutmeg and continue sautéing. Once well blended, add whole tomatoes. Mash tomatoes while cooking on high heat.
4) When sauce begins to thicken, add spinach and mix well. Adjust flavor with salt and pepper. Add cheese and lightly stir.
5) Serve over rice in bowls.

Pork Stroganoff Donburi

Flour coating entraps flavor and keeps the meat tender

Photo on page 19

You're probably thinking that a creamy dish like this is better suited to bread, but just try it with rice. It's a surprisingly nice match. This donburi caused the photography staff to do a double take. Seriously.

Ingredients (Serves 2)

7 oz (200 g) pork tenderloin
1/2 pack each *maitake*, king oyster, and *shimeji* mushrooms
1 tsp olive oil
1 Tbsp butter
Flour, for dredging
Salt and pepper, to taste
1 clove garlic, minced
2 Tbsp white wine
4/5 C (200 ml) fresh cream
1/5 C (50 ml) milk
1/2 tsp wholegrain mustard
2 servings steaming hot rice
Minced parsley, to taste

Instructions

1) Cut pork into 2/5" (1 cm) slices. Shred maitake and king oyster mushrooms into bite-size pieces and break up shimeji mushrooms into small clusters.
2) Add olive oil to a heated pan and melt butter in oil. Coat meat in flour and place in pan. Sprinkle with salt and pepper, cover, and cook on medium heat until browned. Turn over.
3) Once both sides are browned, add garlic and stir-fry. Move meat to side of pan. Add mushrooms to the open space in pan and stir-fry on high heat. When mushrooms are tender, mix everything together and add wine. Stir-fry briefly, add milk and cream, and simmer on medium low heat.
4) When sauce begins to thicken, add mustard and mix. Add salt and pepper to taste.
5) Serve over rice in bowls. Sprinkle with parsley and, if desired, pepper.

Note

It can take a while to add the meat to the pan, so I suggest you turn off the heat to keep the meat from charring. Just a little hint.

Super Sesame Chicken Donburi

Roasty toasty sesame will whet your appetite

Recipe on page 26

Chicken Meatloaf Donburi
Serve with flair and eat with gusto

Recipe on page 26

Coconut Milk
Curry Donburi
**Simple Thai curry turned
easy donburi topping**
Recipe on page 27

Loco Moco Donburi
Nice and spicy chicken burger

Recipe on page 27

Super Sesame Chicken Donburi

Extra oil is the secret to a delicious flavor

Photo on page 22

Chicken roasted until the skin is crackly and crispy, plus a heap of sesame—you can't beat that robust flavor. Juicy roasted peppers are a perfect complement. And don't forget to add the sauce from the pan.

Ingredients (Serves 2)

2 chicken thighs (12 to 14 oz (350 to 400 g) total)
1 green bell pepper
A: 3 to 4 Tbsp roasted white sesame seeds
   2 Tbsp each sake (or cooking wine) and water
   1 Tbsp + 1 tsp soy sauce
   1 Tbsp mirin (sweet cooking wine)
   1/2 Tbsp sugar
2 Tbsp vegetable oil
2 servings steaming hot rice

Instructions

1) Remove fat from chicken and cut slits along the meat side about 2/5" (1 cm) apart. Gently poke holes in side with skin. Quarter green pepper lengthwise. Combine mixture A.
2) Add 1 Tbsp oil to a heated pan and lay chicken in pan, skin side down. Cover and cook until lightly browned. Turn over and cover again. Cook slowly.
3) When chicken is almost done, add green peppers and cook just until browned. Remove peppers.
4) Once chicken is thoroughly cooked, soak up excess liquid and oil with a paper towel. Turn skin side down. Add 1 Tbsp oil and cook on high heat until skin is crispy. Pour in mixture A and coat chicken. Remove and cut into bite-size pieces.
5) Serve rice in bowls and top with chicken and green peppers. Add juices from the pan.

Chicken Meatloaf Donburi

The more you knead the meat, the more the need to eat

Photo on page 23

You may have never heard of chicken meatloaf, but try this oversized version of traditional Japanese chicken meat-balls, called *tsukune*, and you'll fall in love. The flavorful juices captured in this generously sized meatloaf trickle down into the rice. It's mouth-wateringly delicious.

Ingredients (Serves 2)

5 1/4 oz (150 g) ground chicken
1 3/4 oz (50 g) boiled bamboo shoots
1 fresh shiitake mushroom
1/4 onion
A: 1/2 nub ginger, minced
   1 egg yolk
   1/2 Tbsp sugar
   1 tsp each soy sauce, mirin (sweet cooking wine), and sake (or cooking wine)
   Pinch salt
   Japanese (*sansho*) pepper, to taste
2 Tbsp vegetable oil
B: 1 C (200 ml) water
   1 1/2 Tbsp soy sauce
   1 Tbsp each mirin (sweet cooking wine), sake (or cooking wine), and sugar
   1 Tbsp potato (or corn) starch
1/4 bunch *komatsuna* (or sub. mustard greens)
2 servings steaming hot rice
Japanese (*sansho*) pepper, to taste

Instructions

1) Dice bamboo shoots and shiitake into 1/5" (5 mm) cubes. Mince onion.
2) Place ground chicken and mixture A in a bowl and knead well by hand. When meat turns sticky, add vegetables from step 1 and mix well. Rub a small amount of oil onto hands, divide meat in half, and shape into two large ovals.
3) Pour oil into a heated pan and add meatloaves. Cover and cook on medium heat until well browned. Turn over and cook other side. Remove meatloaves from pan.
4) Lightly wipe off pan and add mixture B. Bring to a boil. Add *komatsuna* (or mustard greens) with root ends removed and simmer on medium heat. When *komatsuna* is tender, return meatloaf to pan and simmer briefly.
5) Serve over rice in bowls. Add Japanese pepper, if desired.

Notes

- Knead seasoned meat thoroughly for a delicious, chewy texture.
- Check for doneness by poking a skewer into the center of the meatloaf. If the juice that comes out is clear—or no juice comes out at all—the meatloaf is ready. If the juice is cloudy, the meatloaf needs to cook more.

Coconut Milk Curry Donburi

Chinese chili paste works wonders on your taste buds

Photo on page 24

Thanks to the coconut milk, this dish is simultaneously spicy and mild. And thanks to the chili paste and garlic, it's an impeccable match for rice.

Ingredients (Serves 2)

5 1/4 oz (150 g) chicken breast
6 shrimp or prawns
1 stalk celery
1 red bell pepper
1 bunch cilantro
1 clove garlic, minced
1 nub ginger, minced
1 Tbsp sesame oil
1/2 to 1 Tbsp Doubanjiang (Chinese chili paste)
1 tsp curry powder
1/2 can (7 oz (200 g)) coconut milk
1 tsp sugar
Nam pla (Thai fish sauce), salt and pepper to taste
2 servings steaming hot rice

Instructions

1) Cut chicken breast into 2/5" (1 cm) slices. Devein shrimp. Skin celery with a peeler, cut into thin diagonal slices and shred leaves. Cut bell pepper lengthwise into thin strips. Chop cilantro.
2) In a heated pan add sesame oil, garlic, ginger, and Doubanjiang. Sauté on low heat until fragrant. Add chicken. Sprinkle on salt and pepper and stir-fry on high heat. Add shrimp when chicken is mostly cooked and sauté.
3) When shrimp is cooked, add celery and sauté until tender. Add bell pepper and mix, coating evenly with oil. Add curry powder and coconut milk and simmer on medium heat. When sauce begins to thicken, add sugar. Add nam pla, salt and pepper to taste.
4) Serve over rice in bowls. Garnish with cilantro.

Loco Moco Donburi

Steamed hamburger delight

Photo on page 25

Gooey egg yolk dripping over a juicy burger fresh from the pan, sitting atop a bowl of freshly steamed hot rice—this is a hot and delicious treat. It's Hawaiian fast food meets Japanese home cooking.

Ingredients (Serves 2)

7 oz (200 g) ground chicken
1/4 onion
A: 1/2 Tbsp vegetable oil
   Pinch salt
   Dash each pepper and chili powder
   Plenty of nutmeg
2 eggs
Water, as needed
1/2 Tbsp vegetable oil (for eggs)
1/2 Tbsp vegetable oil (for burgers)
B: 1/2 C (100 ml) water
   1 1/2 Tbsp ketchup
   1 Tbsp each Worcestershire sauce, sake (or cooking wine), and butter
   1 tsp soy sauce
2 servings steaming hot rice
Pepper, to taste

Instructions

1) Mince onion. Thoroughly mix ground chicken and mixture A in a bowl. Add onion and mix again. Divide in half and shape into two large ovals.
2) Make half-cooked sunny-side up eggs. See page 9 for reference.
3) Add oil to a heated pan and add burgers. Cook on medium heat until browned and pour in water until burgers are half covered. Cover and steam on medium heat. Poke with a skewer; if clear juice comes out, the meat is cooked.
4) When water has evaporated, remove hamburgers from pan. Add mixture B and simmer on medium heat until thickened. Return burgers to pan and coat with sauce.
5) Serve rice in bowls and top with burger and egg. Pour on sauce remaining in pan. Sprinkle with pepper, if desired.

Notes

- Loco moco is a common dish served at casual eateries in Hawaii. It consists of a burger with gravy and sunny-side up egg on top of rice.
- Here I introduced a clever way of cooking burgers well done without burning them: steaming. You may think the flavor would get watered down, but trust me and try it.

Spicy Chunky Tofu Donburi
A bold take on tofu
Recipe on page 30

Pork Kimchi Donburi
Sweet and spicy kimchi on rice
Recipe on page 30

Spicy Chunky Tofu Donburi

Be sure to drain the tofu well

Photo on page 28

No time for cutting or chopping? Try this simple stir-fry sensation. Just whip out the wok. Put the tofu in the pan whole and break it up as you cook. It can't get any simpler. The glistening spicy sauce dripping from the edges of the tofu will make your mouth water.

Ingredients (Serves 2)

1 small block firm tofu
3 1/2 oz (100 g) ground pork
1 bunch garlic chives
1/2 bunching onion (or sub. green onion or leek)
1 clove garlic
1 nub ginger
1 Tbsp + 1 tsp sesame oil
A: 1 Tbsp each red miso and sake (or cooking wine)
   1/2 Tbsp each soy sauce, oyster sauce, and Doubanjiang (Chinese chili paste)
   Japanese (*sansho*) pepper, to taste
1/4 C (50 ml) water
2 servings steaming hot rice

Instructions

1) Drain tofu for about 15 minutes. Cut garlic chives into 3" (7 cm) lengths and bunching onion into thin rounds. Mince ginger and garlic. Combine mixture A.
2) Pour 1 Tbsp sesame oil into a heated pan and sauté bunching onion, ginger, and garlic on low heat until fragrant. Add sliced pork and turn heat to high. Crumble meat as you stir-fry.
3) When meat is mostly browned, add mixture A and stir-fry to coat. Add tofu and water. Mix, breaking tofu into chunks of desired size with a spatula. Cook until piping hot and add garlic chives. Stir quickly and remove from heat. Add additional 1 tsp sesame oil for a finishing touch.
4) Serve over rice in bowls.

Notes

- In the photo on page 28 I used Sichuan pepper instead of Japanese pepper. Use Sichuan pepper for an authentic Chinese flavor. Look for it at Asian markets. If you find it sold as whole peppercorns, finely chop with a knife. But be careful—it's spicy!
- Drain tofu by wrapping it in a paper towel and pressing it with a plate for 10 to 15 minutes. Draining the tofu well eliminates the need to thicken the sauce with cornstarch. If you're in a hurry, cooking tofu in boiling water for 2 to 3 minutes will toughen it up.

Pork Kimchi Donburi

Cook meat well before adding kimchi

Photo on page 29

Pork kimchi is a dish characterized by its sharp, spicy flavor, but I suggest adding a bit of sweetness to make it more suitable for rice. Add mushrooms for fuller flavor and more volume.

Ingredients (Serves 2)

5 1/4 oz (150 g) thinly sliced pork shoulder
1/2 pack *enoki* mushrooms
1/2 bunch spring onions (or scallions)
5 1/4 oz (150 g) Napa cabbage kimchi
1 Tbsp + 1 tsp sesame oil
1 clove garlic, 1 nub ginger
Salt and pepper, to taste
1 Tbsp sake (or cooking wine)
1/2 Tbsp each soy sauce and mirin (sweet cooking wine)
1 Tbsp roasted white sesame seeds
2 servings steaming hot rice

Instructions

1) Cut pork into bite-size pieces. Remove root end from mushrooms and shred. Cut onions to 2" (5 cm) segments and mince ginger and garlic. Cut kimchi into bite-size pieces.
2) Pour 1 Tbsp sesame oil in a heated pan and sauté ginger and garlic on low heat until fragrant. Add pork and lightly season with salt and pepper. Stir-fry on high heat until browned.
3) Add mushrooms. Cook until mushrooms are tender, then add scallions and kimchi. Stir-fry. Add sake, soy sauce, and mirin, stir, and finish with additional 1 tsp sesame oil.
4) Serve over rice in bowls.

Korean-Style Seasoned Cabbage recipe on page 84

Noodle Scramble Donburi
Rinse the boiled noodles thoroughly
Photo on page 32

In the islands of Okinawa in the far south of Japan, there's a delicious dish made with thin wheat noodles. I like to eat mine with rice, so I made it into a donburi. Make it salty and top with plenty of pepper.

Ingredients (Serves 2)
3 1/2 oz (100 g) thinly sliced pork belly
3 1/2 oz (100 g) *somen* (Japanese vermicelli)
1 bunching onion (or sub. green onion or leek)
1/3 carrot, peeled
1 clove garlic
1 nub ginger
1 Tbsp sesame oil
1 C bean sprouts
1 Tbsp sake (or cooking wine)
1/2 tsp soy sauce
Salt and pepper, to taste
2 to 3 Tbsp *sakura* shrimp (dried dwarf shrimp. Or sub. salad shrimp)
2 servings steaming hot rice

Instructions
1) Cut pork into large bite-size pieces. Cut bunching onion diagonally into 1/8" (3 mm) slices. Julienne carrot, and mince garlic and ginger.
2) Cook *somen* (or vermicelli) noodles as directed on package and rinse thoroughly in running water to cool. Drain well.
3) Pour sesame oil in a heated pan and sauté garlic and ginger on low heat until fragrant. Add pork and lightly season with salt and pepper. Stir-fry on high heat.
4) Add bunching onion when meat is browned. When bunching onion is lightly charred, add carrots and bean sprouts. Stir-fry.
5) When carrot is tender, add noodles. Stir-fry until noodles are coated evenly with oil and add sake. Stir-fry quickly, add soy sauce, and mix. Add salt and pepper to taste, then add shrimp and mix quickly.
6) Serve over rice in bowls. Sprinkle with pepper.

Noodle Stir-fry Donburi
Cook eggs quickly on high heat for a creamy finish
Photo on page 33

In the western region of Japan, there's a meal consisting of *udon* noodles with rice. The dish is popular with people of all ages. This is the Kentaro version of noodles and rice.

Ingredients (Serves 2)
3 1/2 oz (100 g) thinly sliced pork shoulder
1/4 head cabbage
2" (5 cm) carrot, peeled
1 to 2 Tbsp + 1 tsp vegetable oil
Salt and pepper, to taste
2 servings *yakisoba* (soft egg noodles) (1 dry C, cooked)
1/4 to 1/2 C (50 to 100 ml) water
Tonkatsu, *yakisoba* or Worcestershire sauce, to taste
2 eggs
Pinch each salt and sugar
1 Tbsp butter
2 servings steaming hot rice
Dried seaweed flakes, to taste
Red pickled ginger, to taste

Instructions
1) Cut pork and cabbage into bite-size pieces. Slice carrot into narrow rectangles.
2) Add 1 to 2 Tbsp oil to a heated pan and stir-fry pork on high heat. When lightly browned, add cabbage and carrot, lightly sprinkle with salt and pepper, and stir-fry.
3) When cabbage is tender, add noodles and water. Break up noodles as you stir-fry. When noodles are separated and water has evaporated, add sauce to taste.
4) Lightly beat egg and mix in salt and sugar. Heat 1 tsp oil in a separate pan. Add butter and melt. Pour egg into melted butter. Cook on high heat and mix briskly with cooking chopsticks to make creamy half-cooked scrambled egg.
5) Serve rice in bowls and top with stir-fried noodles and egg. Top with dried seaweed flakes and red pickled ginger.

Noodle Scramble Donburi
**An irresistible combination of
garlic and pepper**
Recipe on page 31

Noodle Stir-fry Donburi

**Rice dripping with delicious
sweet and spicy sauce with creamy egg**

Recipe on page 31

Just whip it up with whatever pan you can find. After all, it's a donburi.

Don't think that you need any special tools for making a donburi. The opposite is true, really. Because it's donburi you're making. It seems strange to purchase a collection of special pans and gadgets for the sake of making donburi. It just doesn't fit with the image of donburi as a modern, easy and casual meal.

That's why it makes sense to use everyday utensils and ordinary skills. Donburi are meant to be whipped up in one second and eaten the next, so it's silly to go to the trouble of getting out some specialized gadget or pan.

The only specialized tool for making donburi in the first place is a big flattened ladle-like pan for making simmered egg sauce. I guess that shows how important simmered egg sauce is when it comes to making donburi. The special egg sauce pan has a perpendicular handle and its own accompanying lid, and it's ingeniously designed so that you can just slide your half-cooked creamy egg sauce right on top of the rice in one smooth motion. But it isn't absolutely necessary. Of course, if you already have one, go ahead and use it. But if you don't have it, no problem. I don't have one either.

I usually make a single serving of simmered egg sauce in a generic 6" (14 cm) saucepan. All the egg sauce you see photographed in this book was made with such a pan. A normal saucepan is too deep to just slide the egg on top of the rice, but that's not a big problem. Just split the simmered egg in the middle and place it onto the rice one half at a time with a spatula or large spoon. Problem solved. This is how I serve up all my simmered egg sauce. If you place each portion carefully so the edges are matched, there's no way of telling it isn't all in one piece. And you'll break it up when you eat it anyway, so it doesn't really make a big difference. If you're cooking for four you can use a frying pan or any pot, enamel or stainless steel or other, for making simmered egg sauce. So, as I said, that perpendicular handled egg sauce pan is unnecessary.

Grab whatever ingredients you can find, whatever pan you can get your hands on, whip it up, then eat it up. That's my philosophy when making donburi.

Donburi Classics

There are all kinds of unusual and original donburi, but you just can't beat the classics.
Tempura, pan-fried chicken, Chinese stir-fry, and of course all the simmered egg sauce classics.
You can't have a recipe book on donburi without the classics.
You can eat them again and again and never get sick of them.

Tempura Donburi

Fried light and crispy and steeped in plenty of sweet and salty sauce

Serve with Lightly Pickled Veggies and Home-Style Miso Soup.
Making your own Tempura Donburi at home has various advantages. Nice and plump battered shrimp, crispy and satisfying mouthfuls of vegetables. It's no wonder that the character for *tem* in *tempura* means "heaven."

Dip freshly fried tempura in yummy sauce!

Ingredients (Serves 2)

4 large shrimp (Taisho, black tiger, etc.)
1/4 *kabocha* (aka Japanese pumpkin.
　　Or sub. pumpkin or buttercup squash)
1/2 pack *maitake* mushrooms
A: 1 1/2 C (300 ml) flour
　　1 C (200 ml) water
　　10 ice cubes
Oil for deep frying (The best temperature for frying is between 350° and 375°)
4 *shiso* leaves (or sub. basil or mint leaves)
B: 1/2 C (100 ml) water
　　1 Tbsp soy sauce
　　1 Tbsp each sugar and mirin (sweet cooking wine)
2 servings steaming hot rice

Instructions

1) Shell shrimp, leaving tails, and devein. To keep from curling when fried, split open underside in 3 places by hand and stretch straight (see photo 1).
Cut *kabocha* into 1/8" (3 mm) crescent slices. Shred *maitake* into bite-size clusters.

2) In a bowl combine mixture A, leaving some clumps of flour (see photo 2).

3) Heat 1 1/5" (3 cm) oil on medium heat. Dip each ingredient in batter (mixture A) and fry, keeping heat at medium high. Let fry undisturbed until batter begins to stiffen, then turn over occasionally. Fry slowly, allowing moisture to fully evaporate (see photos 3 and 4). Fry in the following order: *kabocha*, *maitake*, *shiso* leaves, then shrimp.

4) Bring mixture B to boil in a saucepan and dip the freshly fried tempura in the heated sauce one at a time (see photo 5). Serve rice in bowls and top with tempura.

Lightly Pickled Veggies recipe on page 86
Home-Style Miso Soup recipe on page 94

1　2　3　4　5

Pan-fried Chicken Donburi

Getting the crispy skin side just right is the key to success
Serve with Grilled Eggplant

Cook chicken thigh meat whole and then cut. That way, the rich flavor is kept inside until the very last moment. Pan-fried chicken with a delicious coating of sauce and a sprinkling of fragrant pepper is an irresistible treat.

Use a generous layer of roasted seaweed on top of the rice

Ingredients (Serves 2)

2 boneless chicken thighs (12 to 14 oz (350 to 400 g) total)
1/2 pack Japanese sweet peppers (*shishito*. Or sub. 1 bell pepper or sweet frying peppers)
2 Tbsp vegetable oil
Salt and pepper, to taste
A: 2 Tbsp water
  1 Tbsp each miso and mirin (sweet cooking wine)
  1/2 Tbsp soy sauce
2 servings steaming hot rice
Roasted seaweed, to taste
Japanese (*sansho*) pepper, to taste

Instructions

1) Remove fat from chicken and poke several holes in skin side with a knife (see photo 1). Make slicing cuts into skinless side about 2/5" (1 cm) apart (see photo 2). Remove stems of peppers and poke random holes with a skewer so they won't burst open when frying.
2) Put 1/2 Tbsp oil in a heated pan and add peppers. Sprinkle with salt and pepper and sauté on high heat. Remove from pan when lightly browned.
3) Lightly wipe frying pan and add 1 Tbsp oil. Place chicken thighs in pan, skin side down. Sprinkle with salt and pepper, cover, and cook on medium heat. Once browned, turn over. Cover again and cook slowly on medium heat. Siphon excess juices and oil from pan with a paper towel while cooking (see photo 3).
4) Once chicken is cooked through, turn skin side down once more. Pour in 1/2 Tbsp oil around the edge of pan and cook on high heat until skin is crispy. Siphon off excess fat again and pour in mixture A. Coat both sides well (see photo 4).
5) Cut chicken into bite-size pieces. Serve rice in bowls and cover with shredded pieces of roasted seaweed (see photo 5), then top with broiled chicken and peppers. Sprinkle with Japanese *sansho* pepper.

Grilled Eggplant recipe on page 89

2

3   4   5

1   2   3

Chinese Stir-fry Donburi

Don't forget the finishing touch of sesame oil
Serve with *Harusame* Salad

Chinese stir-fry is usually characterized by a salty flavor, but for donburi be sure to use plenty of oyster sauce. The strong, rich flavor is a great match for rice. If you can make starch paste without any clumps, you have mastered this dish.

Turn off heat when adding starch paste

Ingredients (Serves 2)

3 1/2 oz (100 g) thinly sliced pork shoulder
1 1/2 oz (45 g) canned quail eggs
      (appx. 5 eggs)
1/8 head Napa cabbage
2" (5 cm) carrot, peeled
1/2 bunch garlic chives
1 heaping Tbsp (appx. 3 pieces) dried
   cloud ear or wood ear mushroom
1 clove garlic
1 nub ginger
A: 1 C (200 ml) water
   Dash soy sauce
   1 Tbsp each sake (or cooking wine) and
     oyster sauce
B: 1 Tbsp potato (or corn) starch
   2 Tbsp water
1 Tbsp + 1 tsp sesame oil
Salt and pepper, to taste
2 servings steaming hot rice

Instructions

1) Cut pork into large bite-size pieces. Divide Napa cabbage into stems and leaves. Chop leaves roughly and slice stems into 2" (5 cm) wide strips. Cut carrot into thin strips. Slice chives to a length of 2" (5 cm). Reconstitute cloud ear mushrooms by soaking in water. Mince garlic and ginger. Drain quail eggs.
2) Combine mixtures A and B in separate bowls.
3) Pour 1 Tbsp sesame oil into a heated pan and sauté garlic and ginger on low heat (see photo 1) until fragrant. Add pork, sprinkle with salt and pepper, and stir-fry on high heat (see photo 2).

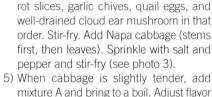

4

4) When meat is lightly browned, add carrot slices, garlic chives, quail eggs, and well-drained cloud ear mushroom in that order. Stir-fry. Add Napa cabbage (stems first, then leaves). Sprinkle with salt and pepper and stir-fry (see photo 3).
5) When cabbage is slightly tender, add mixture A and bring to a boil. Adjust flavor with salt and pepper. Turn off heat. Mix B thoroughly, pour into stir-fry with a circular motion, and stir together quickly with a wooden spoon (see photos 4 and 5). Cook briefly on medium heat, stirring constantly, to thicken sauce.
6) Serve rice in bowls. Top with stir-fry and additional 1 tsp of sesame oil.

Harusame Salad recipe on page 87

5

Chicken and Egg Donburi

Juicy chicken bathing in creamy egg

Delicious chicken makes or breaks this donburi. But that doesn't mean you have to buy brand-name poultry. Your average bird is plenty tender and juicy. Just cut into large pieces and enjoy the melt-in-your-mouth goodness.

1   2   3   4

A saucepan is all you need to whip up this delight!

Ingredients (Serves 2)
1 boneless chicken thigh (8 3/4 oz, or 250 g)
2 eggs
1 bunching onion (or sub. green onion or leek)
A: 1/2 C (100 ml) water
    2 Tbsp mirin (sweet cooking wine)
    1 Tbsp each soy sauce and sugar
2 servings steaming hot rice

Instructions
1) Slice bunching onion diagonally to 2/5" (1 cm) segments. Remove fat from chicken and cut into bite-size pieces. Lightly beat eggs just enough to mix yolk and whites. Combine mixture A.
2) Make one serving at a time. Add half of mixture A to a small saucepan and bring to boil on medium heat. Add half of bunching onion and chicken and cover with lid slightly askew (see photo 1). Simmer.
3) Once chicken is cooked, add half of eggs in a circular motion, trickling over chopsticks (or fork) as you pour. Cover immediately and simmer on low heat for 30 seconds (see photos 2 and 3). Turn off heat and leave lid on to steam for 20 seconds.
4) Serve rice in a bowl and top with creamy chicken and egg (see photo 4). Repeat for remaining serving.

Creamy Egg Donburi

Be picky about your eggs.

It goes without saying that this donburi needs good eggs. So loosen your purse strings and buy high-quality eggs. That is the first step to making a successful Creamy Egg Donburi. The second step is getting the half-cooked egg to just the right degree of creaminess. Pour egg in a circular motion and cover pan. Count to 30, then turn off heat. Count to 20, and it's done. The last 50 seconds are the key.

A piece of cake to make with Japanese noodle sauce!
Ingredients (Serves 2)
2 eggs
8 slices fish cake 1/5" (5 mm) thick (*kamaboko*. Or sub. imitation crab stick, 2 legs, sliced on the bias)
1/4 onion
1/4 bunch mitsuba leaves (or sub. watercress or chervil)
1/2 C (100 ml) diluted Japanese noodle sauce (see Reference Guide)
2 servings steaming hot rice

Instructions
1) Cut *kamaboko* (or imitation crab legs) in two to three pieces lengthwise. Thinly slice onion along the grain. Cut *mitsuba* (or watercress) leaves to 2" (5 cm) lengths. Lightly whisk eggs.
2) Make one serving at a time. Bring half of noodle sauce to boil on medium heat. Add half of onion and *kamaboko* (or crab legs) and bring to boil again. When onion is tender, add half of eggs in a circular motion, trickling over chopsticks (or fork) as you pour. Sprinkle in *mitsuba* (or watercress) leaves and cover immediately. Simmer on low heat for 30 seconds and turn off heat. Leave covered to steam for 20 seconds.
3) Serve rice in a bowl and top with above. Repeat for remaining serving.

Shrimp and Fried Tofu Donburi

The scent of ginger is tantalizing

This donburi is created with average ingredients commonly found in a Japanese home. It may not seem like much, but take a closer look. It is actually a well-balanced and nutritional one-dish meal. I recommend adding a little extra sweetness to the sauce.

Lower heat once egg is added!
Ingredients (Serves 2)
2 eggs
4 to 6 large shrimp (Taisho, black tiger, etc.)
1/2 block thick fried tofu (*atsuage*. Or sub. Tofu Cutlet)
1 bunch garlic chives
1 nub ginger
1 C (200 ml) diluted Japanese noodle sauce (see Reference Guide)
1/2 Tbsp sugar
2 servings steaming hot rice

Instructions
1) Shell shrimp and remove tails. Slice back and spread open. Devein and rinse in running water. Pat dry. Cut chives into 2" (5 cm) pieces. Cut fried tofu in half and cut into 2/5" (1 cm) wide pieces. Mince ginger.
2) Make one serving at a time. Pour half of noodle sauce, sugar, and ginger in a small saucepan and bring to boil on medium heat. Add half of shrimp and fried tofu, cover, and simmer for 3 minutes. Add garlic chives in the last 20 seconds and cover again.
3) When shrimp is cooked and garlic chives are tender, add 1 lightly beaten egg in a circular motion, trickling over chopsticks (or fork) as you pour. Replace lid immediately and simmer on low heat for 30 seconds. Turn off heat and leave covered to steam for 20 seconds.
4) Serve rice in a bowl and top with above. Repeat for remaining serving.

Delicious Fish

Fish want to be made into donburi, too.
Tofu and pork cutlets and shrimp
have all joined the cast of donburi
favorites. Why not fish?
There's no reason not to add
them to the roll call.
So here they are—this
chapter is all about fish.
Dear fish, how does it feel
to be on the big stage?

Donburi

Tuna Avocado Donburi

Enjoy the powerful
aroma of wasabi!
Serve with
Cilantro Salad and
Curry Soup with
Bacon and Celery.

Recipe on page 50

Butter Yellowtail
Teriyaki Donburi
**Butter adds a heart-melting
richness**

Recipe on page 50

Japanese Breakfast Donburi
Savory, refreshing, and a great match for rice
Serve with Spicy Shrimp and Soybean Sprouts

Recipe on page 51

48

Marinated Sashimi Donburi

The scent of sesame will keep you coming back for more
Serve with Stir-fried Dried Daikon

Recipe on page 51

Tuna Avocado Donburi

Avocado pits keep the avocado from turning brown

Photo on page 46

There's no cooking involved in this donburi topping, just cutting and mixing. Creamy tuna and avocado wrapped in the aroma of wasabi mayonnaise. It's very simple, but the sum total is nothing short of celestial.

Ingredients (Serves 2)

1/2 slab (appx. 2 1/2 oz) sushi-grade raw tuna
1 avocado
A: 1 Tbsp soy sauce
   1/2 to 1 Tbsp lemon juice
   1 tsp mayonnaise
   Wasabi, to taste (appx. 1/2 tsp)
2 servings steaming hot rice

Instructions

1) Cut tuna into 4/5" (2 cm) cubes. Pierce avocado with knife and slice around pit lengthwise. Break in half, peel, and remove pit. Cut into 4/5" (2 cm) cubes. Reserve pit.
2) Combine mixture A in a bowl. Add avocado and tuna and toss well. Add avocado pit to keep avocado from losing its attractive color.
3) Serve rice in bowls and top with tuna and avocado. Don't serve the pit.

Cilantro Salad recipe on page 91
Curry Soup with Bacon and Celery recipe on page 95

Butter Yellowtail Teriyaki Donburi

Coat with sauce while cooking rather than marinating

Photo on page 47

As butter melts away in the steaming hot sauce, a rich aroma fills your nostrils. Thick, rich, sweet and spicy sauce with savory butter is a mouth-watering combination. You'll hardly be able to wait to get a hold of some chopsticks and start digging into this tempting treat.

Ingredients (Serves 2)

2 large cuts yellowtail
   (or sub. mahi mahi)
1/2 bunch spring onions (or scallions)
A: 2 Tbsp mirin (sweet cooking wine)
   1 Tbsp each soy sauce, sugar, sake
      (or cooking wine), and water
1 1/2 Tbsp vegetable oil
2 servings steaming hot rice
1 Tbsp butter

Instructions

1) Cut off root ends of spring onions (or scallions). Combine mixture A.
2) Add 1/2 Tbsp oil to a heated pan and stir-fry onions briskly on high heat just until lightly charred. Remove from pan.
3) Wipe pan and reheat. Add 1 Tbsp oil. Pat dry yellowtail (or mahi mahi) filets and place in pan. Cover and cook on medium heat. Turn over once lightly browned. Cook until well-done.
4) Add mixture A to pan and coat fish while cooking on high heat.
5) Serve rice in bowls and top with onions and yellowtail. Pour in remaining sauce from pan and add butter on top.

Notes

- The key is to give the fish a good coating of sauce. To do this, pat the fish thoroughly dry before cooking and wipe excess fat from the pan with a paper towel while cooking.
- Teriyaki yellowtail is usually made by marinating the fish before cooking, but the fish burns easily that way. I avoid this problem by coating it with sauce while cooking, as in this recipe.

Japanese Breakfast Donburi

Drain grated daikon thoroughly

Photo on page 48

Dried fish and grated daikon—that's a traditional Japanese breakfast for you. Make it into a donburi, and you have a great meal to satisfy a growling stomach. Sesame oil enhances the flavor of soy sauce for a perfectly balanced flavor.

Ingredients (Serves 2)

2 whole dried fish (horse mackerel, etc.)
1/2 bunch edible chrysanthemum (aka chop suey greens, or sub. spinach)
1 cucumber
A: 2 Tbsp roasted white sesame seeds
   1 Tbsp each sesame oil and soy sauce
   1 tsp sugar
2 servings steaming hot rice
2" (5 cm) segment daikon radish, grated
Soy sauce, to taste

Instructions

1) Grill dried fish well, remove bones, and break up meat into small pieces. Cut off root ends of chrysanthemum (or spinach) and cut into 2" (5 cm) lengths. Halve cucumber lengthwise and cut each half diagonally into 1/8" (3 mm) slices.
2) Combine mixture A in a bowl. Add ingredients from step 1 and toss thoroughly.
3) Serve rice in bowls and top with above. Add grated daikon and sprinkle with soy sauce.

Notes

Lightly squeeze liquid from the grated daikon before adding it to the donburi. If you have time, allow it to drain naturally in a colander.

Spicy Shrimp and Soybean Sprouts recipe on page 84

Marinated Sashimi Donburi

Decorate with large *shiso* leaves

Photo on page 49

Use whatever sashimi you like. The point is adding sesame oil to the sauce. Donburi with marinated toppings are good, but the flavor can get monotonous. Sesame oil is a novel twist.

Ingredients (Serves 2)

2 to 3 servings of sushi-grade fish for sashimi
A: 1 Tbsp soy sauce
   1/2 Tbsp each sesame oil and mirin (sweet cooking wine)
   1/2 to 1 tsp sake (or cooking wine)
2 servings steaming hot rice
5 large *shiso* leaves, julienned (or sub. basil or mint leaves)
Wasabi, to taste

Instructions

1) If sashimi is cut too large, cut into bite-size pieces. Place in a bowl. Add mixture A and toss well. Cover with plastic wrap and refrigerate for 5 minutes.
2) Serve rice in bowls and top with marinated fish. Add remaining marinade to rice bowls and top with *shiso* (or basil) leaves. Add wasabi on the side.

Stir-fried Dried Daikon recipe on page 85

Bonito Bonanza Donburi

Thick slices of bonito with plenty of hot and spicy sauce pack a powerful punch

Recipe on page 54

Sweet and Spicy
Swordfish Donburi

**Add a hint of ginger to
tartar sauce**

Recipe on page 54

Salmon Lettuce
Donburi

**A mouthful of soft lettuce
enhances the flavor of the rice**

Recipe on page 55

Bonito Bonanza Donburi
For a crispy finish, use plenty of oil

Photo on page 52

Use a thick cut of bonito, the kind sold for sashimi. Grill well, and don't worry about overcooking; the bonito is dense so the inside will stay just cool enough. The important thing is to get that hearty, crispy flavor just right. Thick rich sauce complements the flavorful fish and plenty of condiments make this dish a satisfying treat.

Ingredients (Serves 2)
1/2 block sushi-grade raw bonito
    (or sub. tuna)
1 bunching onion (or sub. green onion
    or leek)
10 *shiso* leaves (or sub. basil or mint)
1 nub ginger
1 clove garlic
2 to 3 Tbsp vegetable oil
Dash each salt and pepper
2 Tbsp sesame oil
A: 2 Tbsp sake (or cooking wine)
    1/2 Tbsp each Doubanjiang (Chinese
    chili paste), oyster sauce, and soy
    sauce
2 Tbsp roasted white sesame seeds
2 servings steaming hot rice
Seven-spice (or cayenne) powder,
    to taste

Instructions
1) Cut bunching onion diagonally into thin slices. Julienne ginger and *shiso*. Mince garlic. Pat bonito dry.
2) Add vegetable oil to a heated pan and add bonito. Sprinkle salt and pepper and fry on high heat. Turn over when crispy. Cook all four sides in the same way. Remove from pan and slice into bite-size pieces.
3) Lightly wipe pan and reheat. Add sesame oil and sauté garlic and ginger on low heat until fragrant. Add bunching onion and stir-fry on high heat.
4) When onion is tender, add mixture A, *shiso* leaves, and sesame seeds. Stir-fry well, mixing thoroughly.
5) Serve rice in bowls. Top with fish and sprinkle with seven-spice (or cayenne) powder.

Notes
- Be sure to pat the fish thoroughly dry and use plenty of oil.

Sweet and Spicy Swordfish Donburi
Pat swordfish thoroughly dry

Photo on page 53

Swordfish cooked crispy on the outside, soft and juicy on the inside, with a delicious ginger infusion with homemade tartar sauce. That's what you need to make this donburi successful.

Ingredients (Serves 2)
2 cuts swordfish (appx. 5 oz (150 g)
    each)
1/2 bunch green asparagus
A: 1/2 nub ginger, grated
    1 Tbsp each soy sauce, sake (or cooking
    wine), and mirin (sweet cooking wine)
B: 1 boiled egg, diced
    1 Tbsp minced onion
    1 Tbsp minced pickles
    2 to 3 Tbsp mayonnaise
    1/2 to 1 Tbsp milk
Flour, for dredging
Vegetable oil, as needed
2 servings steaming hot rice
Pepper, to taste

Instructions

1) Pat swordfish dry and cut into 4/5" (2 cm) cubes. Remove root ends of asparagus and peel thick skin from the lower 1/3 of each stem. Cut in half. Combine ingredients for mixtures A and B in separate bowls.
2) Place flour in a bowl and dredge swordfish, coating thoroughly. Heat about 2/5" (1 cm) oil in a pan. Fry asparagus on high heat until tender, then remove.
3) Add swordfish and fry on medium heat. Once surface is crispy, turn over occasionally.
4) When fish is golden brown, wipe excess oil from pan with a paper towel. Add mixture A and coat, cooking on high heat.
5) Serve rice in bowls and top with fish, asparagus, and mixture B. Sprinkle with pepper.

Notes

- Coat swordfish with flour after thoroughly wiping off all excess water. This is an essential step for a crispy, pan-fried finish.
- The ginger goes very well with tartar sauce. You can try adding tartar sauce to other ginger-flavored dishes.

Salmon Lettuce Donburi

Ground sesame and cayenne pepper are an essential finishing touch

Photo on page 53

Large chunks of hand-shredded lettuce become soft on top of steaming hot rice, yet remain slightly crispy. This is only possible with a donburi. Flavored mayonnaise completes the unison of rice and topping.

Ingredients (Serves 2)

2 servings salmon, lightly salted (appx. 3 oz (100 g) each)
3 to 4 leaves lettuce
1 Tbsp sake (or cooking wine)
A: 2 Tbsp ground white sesame seeds
   1 Tbsp mayonnaise
   1/2 Tbsp sesame oil
   1/2 tsp soy sauce
   Pinch sugar
   1 Tbsp lemon juice
   Dash pepper
   Dash grated ginger
Salt, to taste
2 servings steaming hot rice
Cayenne pepper and ground white sesame seeds, to taste

Instructions

1) Break lettuce into large pieces by hand. Boil salmon in water with 1 Tbsp sake added for 3 to 5 minutes until cooked through. Wipe dry and remove skin and bones. Break up into bite-size chunks.
2) Combine mixture A in a bowl and add salmon and lettuce. Toss well. Add salt to taste.
3) Serve rice in bowls and top with salmon and lettuce. Sprinkle with cayenne pepper and ground sesame seeds.

Cha Shao Donburi

The spiciness of the onion is a perfect match for *cha shao*. Serve with Lightly Dressed Tofu and Chicken Soup.

Recipe on page 58

Hungry? Too hungry to wait?
Then bring on the donburi.
When you're in no rush to eat,
when there's time to spare,
when you have tomorrow and
the next day off, then it doesn't
have to be donburi.
But when you want something in a snap,
these spiffy jiffy donburi are just what
your rumbling stomach ordered.

Spiffy Jiffy Donburi

Korean-Style Octopus Donburi

Spice up that rice with Korean hot sauce

Recipe on page 59

Cha Shao Donburi
Thinly slice the bunching onion
Photo on page 56

All you need is 5 minutes. It's really that easy. Bunching onions go so perfectly with *cha shao* that, even though it's so filling, this donburi will leave you hungry for more.

Ingredients (Serves 2)
8 3/4 oz (250 g) Chinese roast pork (*cha shao*)
1 bunching onion (or sub. green onion or leek)
A: 1 tsp each grated garlic and grated ginger
    1 Tbsp sesame oil
    1/2 Tbsp each soy sauce and oyster sauce
    1 tsp Doubanjiang (Chinese chili paste)
    1 Tbsp each roasted black and white sesame
      seeds
2 servings steaming hot rice

Instructions
1) Cut *cha shao* into rectangular blocks and heat in microwave. Cut bunching onion diagonally into thin slices.
2) Combine mixture A in a bowl and add bunching onion and *cha shao* in that order and toss.
3) Serve rice in bowls and top with above.

Lightly Dressed Tofu recipe on page 90
Chicken Soup recipe on page 92

Korean-Style Octopus Donburi
Soft-boiled egg deliciously coats the rice
Photo on page 57

This donburi was created after a trip to Seoul. Octopus coated in spicy gochujang (hot pepper paste) has a great texture and satisfying flavor. In Korea, bibimbap—rice served in a bowl with a topping of seasoned vegetables and meat—was always finished with pine nuts, so I added some here, too.

Ingredients (Serves 2)
10 1/2 oz (300 g) boiled octopus
1/2 C soybean sprouts
1/2 bunch spinach
Pinch salt
A: 1 Tbsp sesame oil
   1/2 Tbsp each gochujang (Korean hot pepper paste), soy sauce, and mirin (sweet cooking wine)
   1 tsp sugar
B: Dash grated garlic
   2 Tbsp ground white sesame seeds
   1 Tbsp sesame oil
   2 pinches each salt and sugar
2 soft-boiled eggs, peeled
Pine nuts, to taste
2 servings steaming hot rice

Instructions
1) Bring water to boil and add a little salt. Briefly boil soybean sprouts for about 30 seconds and remove, then boil spinach for about 15 seconds. Rinse boiled spinach in running water, squeeze dry, and cut to 2" (5 cm) lengths.
2) Chop octopus into bite-size chunks.
3) Combine mixtures A and B in separate bowls. Toss octopus with mixture A and vegetables with mixture B.
4) Roast pine nuts in a pan just until lightly browned. Serve rice in bowls and top with octopus and vegetables. Cut soft-boiled egg in half and place in middle of bowl. Sprinkle with roasted pine nuts. Mix well before eating.

Roasted Seaweed Donburi

**Takes roasted seaweed to a whole new level—
oil is the secret to the rich and luscious flavor**

Recipe on page 62

King Oyster Mushroom and Bacon Donburi

Plump and juicy king oyster mushrooms and crispy bacon— a perfect match for rice! Serve with Spicy Vegetable Soup

Recipe on page 63

Roasted Seaweed Donburi

Mix together as you eat

Photo on page 60

It looks simple to make, and it is. But take one bite, and your eyes will open wide with surprise. It's so amazingly good that I'm sure you'll polish it off quickly. Try this combination of typical Japanese condiments-turned-main dish and you'll want to keep all the ingredients in stock.

Ingredients (Serves 2)

4 large sheets roasted seaweed
A: 1 Tbsp soy sauce
   1/2 Tbsp each vegetable oil and mirin (sweet cooking wine)
1/5 oz (5 g) dried bonito flakes
3 Tbsp baby sardines (*shirasu*)
2 servings steaming hot rice
Chopped spring onions (or sub. scallions), to taste

Instructions

1) Shred roasted seaweed into small pieces. Combine mixture A in a bowl and add roasted seaweed, dried bonito flakes, and baby sardines. Toss well.
2) Serve rice in bowls and top with above. Sprinkle with chopped onions (or scallions).

King Oyster Mushroom and Bacon Donburi

No need for oil when cooking bacon

Photo on page 61

Top freshly cooked rice with the complementary textures of king oyster mushrooms and crunchy bacon. The smoky flavor of bacon and the juiciness of sautéed mushrooms create a sublime harmony.

Ingredients (Serves 2)

6 slices bacon
1 pack king oyster mushrooms
2 cloves garlic
Salt and pepper, to taste
2 Tbsp sake (or cooking wine)
1/2 Tbsp soy sauce
1/2 Tbsp butter
2 servings steaming hot rice

Instructions

1) Shred king oyster mushrooms to about the thickness of your forefinger. Mince garlic.
2) Place bacon in pan and cook slowly on low heat until crispy. Remove from pan.
3) Use fat remaining in pan to sauté garlic on low heat until fragrant. Add king oyster mushrooms and sprinkle salt and pepper. Stir-fry on high heat. When mushrooms are tender, add sake, stir-fry some more, and add soy sauce. Stir to coat and turn off heat. Add butter and stir well.
4) Serve rice in bowls and top with above. Sprinkle with pepper, if desired.

Notes

You don't have to add any oil because the bacon has plenty of fat. This is the best way to cook bacon when you want it good and crispy. Use low to medium heat and take your time to cook both sides. To finish, let the bacon sit on a paper towel to absorb excess fat.

Spicy Vegetable Soup recipe on page 93

Tuna Omelet Donburi
The finishing touch of butter and soy sauce will entice your taste buds
Serve with Cheesy Arugula Salad
Recipe on page 66

Wasabi Salmon Donburi
Plenty of wasabi, onion, and roasted seaweed
Recipe on page 66

Shellfish Stir-fry Donburi

Canned seafood ends up a fulfilling flavor
Serve with Chinese-Style Corn Soup

Recipe on page 67

Curry *Kabayaki* Seafood Donburi

Curry powder transforms
Japanese sweet sauce

Recipe on page 67

Tuna Omelet Donburi
Omelets are easy and fun
Photo on page 64

This is the perfect dish when you just don't feel like making anything fancy. No shopping necessary, just use what you have on hand at home. Half-cooked creamy omelet, butter, and tuna make for a flavorful one-dish meal. The saltiness of canned tuna is just right for rice, too. Take a bite and feel energized.

Ingredients (Serves 2)
6 oz (160 g) canned tuna, in water
1 1/2 Tbsp vegetable oil
A: 1 Tbsp soy sauce
    1/2 Tbsp sweet cooking wine
1 Tbsp mayonnaise
2 eggs
2 servings steaming hot rice
2 tsp butter
Soy sauce to taste

Instructions
1) Combine mixture A. Add 1/2 Tbsp oil to a heated pan and add tuna (with canning liquid). Stir-fry on high heat. When tuna is nice and hot, add mixture A and stir-fry. Turn off heat and add mayonnaise and coat tuna. Remove from pan.
2) Lightly wipe pan, reheat, and add 1 Tbsp oil. Turn heat to medium and break eggs into pan. Stir briskly and spread across pan. When edges start to stiffen but the center is still runny, place tuna in center. Fold edges of egg over tuna and cook until surface is lightly browned. Move to a cutting board and cut in half.
3) Serve rice in bowls and top with omelet. Add a drop of butter and a sprinkle of soy sauce for a finishing touch.

Cheesy Arugula Salad recipe on page 88

Wasabi Salmon Donburi
Use sweet and flavorful red miso
Photo on page 64

Canned salmon is often served with mayonnaise, but miso works well, too. Wasabi takes the flavor to a new level. I like my wasabi to be painfully plentiful. Bunching onion and roasted seaweed also go great with miso.

Ingredients (Serves 2)
5 1/4 oz (150 g) canned salmon
1/2 stalk bunching onion (or sub. green onion
    or leek)
A: 1 Tbsp water
    1/2 Tbsp each red miso and mirin
       (sweet cooking wine)
    Wasabi, to taste
2 servings steaming hot rice
1 large sheet roasted seaweed
1/2 to 1 Tbsp each black and white roasted
    sesame seeds

Instructions
1) Drain liquid from canned salmon, remove any bones and shred fish meat. Slice bunching onion (or leek) into 1/8" (3 mm) rounds.
2) Combine mixture A. Add salmon and bunching onion and toss well.
3) Serve rice in bowls and top with hand-shredded roasted seaweed. Spoon salmon on top and sprinkle with roasted sesame seeds.

Notes
If you use brown miso, increase the amount of mirin or add sugar.

Shellfish Stir-fry Donburi
Flavor with plenty of pepper
Photo on page 65

When you use canned shellfish, you can enjoy the added benefit of the flavorful canning liquid. Canned short-necked clam and scallops are packed with flavor and just the right degree of saltiness, so use all of that scrumptious liquid for a delicious donburi.

Ingredients (Serves 2)
1 3/4 oz (50 g) canned short-neck clam
1 3/4 oz (50 g) canned scallops
1/8 head cabbage
1 clove garlic
1 nub ginger
1 Tbsp sesame oil
1 Tbsp sake (or cooking wine)
Salt and pepper, to taste
2 servings steaming hot rice

Instructions
1) Cut cabbage into bite-size pieces. Mince garlic and ginger. Separate canning liquids from shellfish and combine liquids.
2) Pour sesame oil into a heated pan and sauté garlic and ginger on low heat until fragrant. Add shellfish and stir-fry on high heat until shellfish is coated in oil. Add cabbage and stir-fry.
3) When cabbage is slightly tender, add sake and 3 Tbsp of canning liquid. Stir-fry briskly, adding salt and pepper to taste.
4) Serve rice in bowls and top with above. Sprinkle with pepper.

Chinese-Style Corn Soup recipe on page 92

Curry *Kabayaki* Seafood Donburi
I love those tender but crunchy bamboo shoots!
Photo on page 65

A can of *kabayaki*, or fish broiled in sweet sauce, contains plenty of rich seasonings, so technically it could be turned into a donburi as is. But adding curry powder takes it to the next level and is guaranteed to make it a perfect match for rice.

Ingredients (Serves 2)
1 can Japanese *kabayaki* broiled fish
    (sardine, pike, etc.)
1 small boiled bamboo shoot (appx. 2 1/2 oz (70 g))
1/3 bunch spring onions (or sub. scallions)
1 nub ginger
1 Tbsp sesame oil
Dash each salt and pepper
1 Tbsp sake (or cooking wine)
1 Tbsp curry powder
Soy sauce, to taste
2 servings steaming hot rice

Instructions
1) Separate fish and canning sauce. Cut bamboo shoot into 1/5" (5 mm) slices and cut spring onions into 2" (5 cm) lengths. Mince ginger.
2) Pour oil into a heated pan and sauté ginger on low heat until fragrant. Add bamboo shoot and fish in that order. Sprinkle salt and pepper and stir-fry until everything is coated with oil.
3) Add scallions and stir-fry. When scallions are tender, add sake and stir briskly. Add curry powder and all of the canning sauce. Coat well and adjust flavor with soy sauce.
4) Serve rice in bowls and top with above.

Veggie Power

As a side dish, vegetables can be boring.
But put them on top of a bowl of rice
and suddenly vegetables become
amazingly appetizing.
Munch on rice and enjoy a healthy variety
of vegetables at the same time.
Delicious and nutritious!
That's veggie power for you.

Donburi

Ratatouille Donburi

The delicious vegetable
flavor seeps straight
into the rice
Serve with Nutty Cheese
Salad and Julienned
Vegetable Soup

Recipe on page 70

Miso Sauté Donburi

Savor the delicious combination of crunchy peppers and chewy gizzards

Recipe on page 69

Ratatouille Donburi
Don't overcook—let the vegetables keep their shape

Photo on page 68

Ratatouille is a great way to make the most of the summer harvest. Packed with the rich flavor of various vegetables and drenched in refreshingly tangy simmered tomatoes, it's hard to believe that something this good is also nutritious. It's like topping a bowl of rice with sun-blessed goodness.

Ingredients (Serves 2)
2 sausages
1/2 zucchini
1/2 onion
1/2 stalk celery
1 small tomato
1 small yellow bell pepper
2 cloves garlic
2 red chili peppers
2 Tbsp olive oil
1 C (200 ml) water
1 bouillon cube
7 oz (200 g) canned whole tomatoes
2 Tbsp white wine
Dried oregano, to taste
Salt and pepper, to taste
2 servings steaming hot rice

Instructions
1) Cut zucchini into 2/5" (1 cm) half-moon slices. Dice remaining vegetables into half-inch (1.5 cm) cubes. Mash garlic with flat of knife. Remove stems and seeds of chili peppers and cut in half.
2) In a saucepan sauté garlic and red chili peppers in olive oil on low heat. When fragrant, add sausage and stir-fry on high heat until browned. Add vegetables and stir-fry, coating with oil. Add water and bouillon. Simmer.
3) Bring to boil, then reduce heat to low. Skim off bitter foam that floats to the surface and add canned tomatoes, white wine, and oregano. Simmer until vegetables are soft and tender. Break up tomatoes as they cook. Add salt and pepper to taste.
4) Serve rice in bowls and top with ratatouille.

Notes
- When making ratatouille as a donburi topping, there's no need to simmer until the vegetables dissolve.
- Use plenty of oregano for an authentic Italian flavor.

Nutty Cheese Salad recipe on page 87
Julienned Vegetable Soup recipe on page 94

Miso Sauté Donburi

Cook all at once over high heat

Photo on page 69

I don't know why, but I crave bell peppers. Green bell peppers, with their unique bitterness, are to me the perfect vegetable. And red bell peppers, with their surprising sweetness, are an unexpected delight. Both get more flavorful when cooked with oil.

Ingredients (Serves 2)

5 1/4 oz (150 g) chicken gizzards
1 green bell pepper
1 red bell pepper
A: 1 Tbsp each miso, mirin (sweet cooking wine), sake (or cooking wine), water and roasted white sesame seeds
  Dash grated ginger
1 Tbsp sesame oil
Dash each salt and pepper
2 servings steaming hot rice

Instructions

1) Place gizzards in a bowl, and massage in salt. Rinse in running water and drain thoroughly. Make about three cuts into each with kitchen scissors to facilitate cooking. Slice peppers lengthwise into thin strips. Combine mixture A.
2) Pour sesame oil into a heated pan, add gizzards, and lightly sprinkle with salt and pepper. Stir-fry on high heat until cooked through. Add peppers and stir-fry.
3) When peppers are tender, add mixture A and coat.
4) Serve rice in bowls and top with above.

Spicy Mayonnaise Daikon Salad recipe on page 86

Steamed Veggie and Salmon Donburi

The delicious medley of flavors creates a perfect harmony with rice

Recipe on page 74

Chicken Sukiyaki Donburi

The rice and veggies soak up the meat juices

Recipe on page 74

Maitake Mushroom Stir-fry Donburi

Discover the rich flavor of *maitake* mushrooms in this super easy and well-balanced meal
Serve with Pickled Daikon Salad

Recipe on page 75

Steamed Veggie Salmon Donburi

Cover, simmer for five minutes, and it's done

Photo on page 72

Place salmon in a frying pan, cover with a heap of vegetables, add sauce, and turn on the heat. Miso sauce and vegetable juices combine to create a delicious, luxurious, and all-natural flavor. Slide this masterpiece on top of rice for an irresistible treat.

Ingredients (Serves 2)
4 cuts raw salmon (appx. 3 oz (100 g) each)
1/4 head cabbage
1 bunch garlic chives
2" (5 cm) carrot stick
A: 2 Tbsp sake (or cooking wine)
   1 Tbsp each miso, mirin (sweet cooking wine),
      and sesame oil
   1/2 Tbsp each soy sauce and sugar
   Dash each grated garlic and grated ginger
   1/2 C (100 ml) water
2 servings steaming hot rice
Seven-spice (or cayenne) powder, to taste
Ground white sesame seeds, to taste

Instructions
1) Chop cabbage into bite-size pieces and cut garlic chives to 2" (5 cm) lengths. Slice carrot into narrow strips. Combine mixture A.
2) Arrange salmon in a pan and top with cut vegetables. Pour in mixture A with a circular motion. Cover and cook on high heat for 5 to 7 minutes. When salmon is cooked through and vegetables are tender, stir briskly.
3) Serve rice in bowls and top with above. Sprinkle with seven-spice (or cayenne) powder and sesame seeds.

Notes
This dish is a variation on a traditional favorite in Hokkaido, the northernmost of Japan's main islands. Called *chanchanyaki,* it is characterized by a spicy miso flavor.

Chicken Sukiyaki Donburi

Simmer well, but don't overcook it

Photo on page 72

Technically, you could just top a bowl of rice with leftover sukiyaki. But making sukiyaki with the intention of creating a donburi is a different story.
The veggies are fresh and crunchy, and the sauce is simmered just right. You can't beat the combination of hot-off-the-pan sukiyaki and delicious, freshly cooked rice.

Ingredients (Serves 2)
1 boneless, skinless chicken thigh
1 package *konnyaku* noodles (*shirataki*)
1 bunching onion (or sub. green onion
   or leek)
1/2 bunch edible chrysanthemum
   (or sub. spinach)
1 Tbsp vegetable oil
1 1/2 to 2 Tbsp each soy sauce, sugar,
   and mirin (sweet cooking wine)
2 servings steaming hot rice
2 egg yolks
Pepper, to taste

Instructions

1) Remove fat from chicken and cut into 2/5" (1 cm) wide strips. Place *shirataki* in a colander and rinse under running water, then drain. Slice bunching onion (or leek) diagonally to 2" (5 cm) lengths. Remove root ends of chrysanthemum (or spinach) and cut to 2" (5 cm) lengths.

2) Pour oil into a heated pan and add chicken. Cook on medium high heat until browned and turn over. Cook until both sides are well sautéed.

3) Move chicken to edge of pan and add bunching onion. Cook until browned and add 1 Tbsp each soy sauce, sugar, and mirin. Coat with seasonings and add drained *shirataki*. Simmer. Add chrysanthemum and simmer briefly. Add pepper to taste.

4) Serve rice in bowls and top with sukiyaki. Finish with egg yolk on top.

Notes

- Thoroughly cook the chicken before adding the other ingredients.
- Use high heat after adding the seasonings and simmer all at once. Just watch out for burning around the edges of the pan.
- Arranging each ingredient separately on the rice allows you to enjoy a variety of flavors. This is easier if you keep the ingredients separate in the pan when simmering.

Maitake Mushroom Stir-fry Donburi

Thoroughly cook pork first, then add mushrooms

Photo on page 73

Just pork, *maitake* mushrooms, and green onions. They're all easy-to-use ingredients. Stir-fry them up and you're done—it's that simple. Put it on top of rice and you have a surprisingly satisfying and healthy meal.

Ingredients (Serves 2)

3 1/2 oz (100 g) thinly sliced pork shoulder
1 pack (appx. 2 1/2 oz) *maitake* mushrooms
1 bunch green onions (or sub. scallions)
1 clove garlic
1 nub ginger
1 Tbsp sesame oil
1 Tbsp sake (or cooking wine)
1/2 Tbsp oyster sauce
Salt and pepper, to taste
2 servings steaming hot rice

Instructions

1) Cut pork into bite-size pieces. Break up *maitake* mushrooms into small clusters. Remove roots of green onions and cut into 2" (5 cm) lengths. Mince garlic and ginger.

2) Put sesame oil in a heated pan and sauté garlic and ginger on low heat until fragrant. Add pork and stir-fry on high heat until browned. Add *maitake* mushrooms and stir-fry.

3) When mushrooms are slightly tender, add green onions and stir-fry until coated with oil. Add sake and briefly stir-fry. Add oyster sauce and stir to coat. Adjust flavor with salt and pepper.

4) Serve rice in bowls and top with above. Sprinkle with pepper, if desired.

Pickled Daikon Salad recipe on page 90

Mixed Tempura Donburi
Crispy, juicy goodness
Serve with Seaweed Soup

Recipe on page 78

Eggplant Curry Donburi

A Chinese-style curry with the crunch of celery
Serve with Sesame-Dressed Chicken Cucumber Salad

Recipe on page 78

Asian Cabbage Curry Donburi

A light curry with melt-in-your-mouth tender cabbage
Serve with Butter Sautéed *Kabocha*

Recipe on page 79

Mixed Tempura Donburi
For crispy clusters, fry on medium heat

Photo on page 76

As the crispy-crunchy batter melts in your mouth your taste buds will be overwhelmed with the hearty flavor of burdock and sweetness of onion. The sauce-soaked batter flavors the rice, making for a delicious combination.

Ingredients (Serves 2)
3 1/2 oz (100 g) shelled shrimp
1/2 onion
1/2 burdock root
Vinegar/water solution
A: 1 C (200 ml) flour
   3/4 C (150 ml) water
   Pinch each salt and sugar
Oil for deep frying (The best temperature for frying is 350° to 375°)
B: 1 C (200 ml) diluted Japanese noodle sauce (see Reference Guide)
   1 tsp sugar
2 servings steaming hot rice

Instructions
1) Thinly slice onion lengthwise. Scrub surface of burdock with a brush to remove dirt and shave into long strips with a peeler. Soak in vinegar water for 3 minutes. Drain and pat dry.
2) Combine mixture A in a bowl and whisk until no clumps remain. Add onion, burdock, and shrimp. Coat well.
3) Pour oil into a frying pan 4/5" (2 cm) deep and heat to medium high. Scoop up batter-coated ingredients from step 2 with a spatula and slide into oil. Fry slowly on medium low heat, turning over occasionally once the edges of batter become solid. When batter is golden brown, raise heat to high and fry to a crispy finish.
4) Place mixture B in a saucepan and bring to boil. Add tempura and coat both sides.
5) Serve rice in bowl and top with sauce-soaked tempura. Add remaining sauce, if desired.

Seaweed Soup recipe on page 92

Eggplant Curry Donburi
Eggplant is best when fried in plenty of oil

Photo on page 77

Doubanjiang and oyster sauce are the secret seasonings, and they make for a rich and spicy dish. But thanks to the juicy eggplant and the unique fragrance of celery, the spiciness is not overpowering.

Ingredients (Serves 2)
3 1/2 oz (100 g) ground pork
2 to 3 eggplants (the small Japanese or Chinese variety)
Salt water, for soaking
1 stalk celery
1 clove garlic
1 nub ginger
Oil for deep frying (The best temperature for frying is 350° to 375°)
1 Tbsp sesame oil
Salt and pepper, to taste
1 Tbsp sake (or cooking wine)
A: 1/2 Tbsp oyster sauce
   1 to 2 tsp Doubanjiang (Chinese chili paste)
   1 tsp curry powder
2 servings steaming hot rice

Instructions

1) Peel a striped pattern in eggplant skin and quarter lengthwise. Soak in salt water for 3 minutes, drain, and pat dry. Peel celery with a peeler and cut diagonally into thin slices. Mince garlic and ginger.
2) Fill a pan with oil 4/5" (2 cm) deep and bring to high heat. Fry 1/3 of eggplants at a time on high heat until slightly tender and lightly browned.
3) Set aside fried eggplants and empty pan of oil. Reheat pan, add sesame oil, and sauté garlic and ginger on low heat until fragrant. Add ground pork and sprinkle on salt and pepper. Crumble meat while stir-frying on high heat.
4) When meat is browned, add celery and stir-fry until translucent. Return fried eggplants to pan, add sake (or cooking wine), and briefly stir-fry. Add mixture A and coat. Adjust flavor with salt and pepper.
5) Serve rice in bowls and top with above. Sprinkle with pepper and a small amount of sesame oil.

Sesame-Dressed Chicken Cucumber Salad recipe on page 91

Asian Cabbage Curry Donburi
Thinly slice the stems of Napa cabbage

Photo on page 77

Chop Napa cabbage into large chunks and shiitake mushrooms into generous slices, simmer in Japanese soup stock, and flavor with curry powder for a delicious medley of Asian flavors. Extra tender cabbage soaked in thickened sauce has a nice, friendly flavor that will make you happy.

Ingredients (Serves 2)

3 1/2 oz (100 g) thinly sliced pork shoulder
1 block thick fried tofu (*atsuage*.
  Or sub. Tofu Cutlet, appx. 4 oz)
1/8 head Napa cabbage
2 raw shiitake mushrooms
1 nub ginger
1 Tbsp sesame oil
1 Tbsp sake
2 to 3 Tbsp curry powder
1 2/3 C Japanese soup stock
  (see 3rd note)
A: 2 to 3 Tbsp mirin (sweet cooking wine)
  1 Tbsp soy sauce
  Salt to taste
B: 2 Tbsp potato (or corn) starch
  3 Tbsp water
2 servings steaming hot rice
Roasted white sesame seeds, to taste

Instructions

1) Cut pork into bite-size pieces. Cut fried tofu to 1/6" (5 mm) pieces. Split Napa cabbage into leaves and stems. Chop leaves and cut stems into thin strips 2" (5 cm) long. Quarter shiitake and julienne ginger.
2) Pour sesame oil into a heated pan and cook pork on high heat until lightly browned. Add ginger and stir-fry until fragrant. Add fried tofu, shiitake, cabbage stems, and cabbage leaves in that order as you stir-fry.
3) When vegetables become tender, add sake and stir quickly. Add curry powder and coat. Pour in soup stock and bring to a boil. Remove bitter foam that floats to the surface, turn heat to low, and simmer for 5 minutes.
4) Add mixture A. Adjust flavor with salt as needed and turn off heat. Blend mixture B well and pour into pan. Using large sweeping motions, mix together and turn heat on to medium. Simmer, mixing constantly, until sauce thickens.
5) Serve rice in bowls and top with above. Sprinkle with roasted white sesame seeds.

Notes

- Thinly slicing the stem of the Napa cabbage is a favorite technique of mine which can be used in a variety of recipes.
- Turn off heat when adding starch paste to avoid clumping. Once added, turn heat back on and simmer briefly until the sauce thickens evenly.
- Japanese soup stock: bring water almost to a boil and add a handful of bonito flakes. Simmer for 2 minutes and scoop out flakes with a sieved ladle.

Butter Sautéed *Kabocha* recipe on page 92

Rapini Donburi
Enjoy the cheery flavor and colors of spring
Recipe on page 82

Snack Donburi

These miniature donburi make delightful treats. They come in handy when you want something simple to go with a beer, a healthy helping of side dish or when you just want a quick bite to eat. These light snack donburi are proof yet again that the simplest little dish becomes a masterpiece on top of rice.

Kinpira Lotus Root Donburi
A pleasant, spicy surprise encased in sweet sauce coating
Recipe on page 82

Butter Scallop Donburi

A hint of butter, the scent of pepper, the elegant flavor of soy sauce

Recipe on page 83

Liver Donburi

Taste the wonders of butter + soy sauce

Recipe on page 83

Baby Sardine Donburi

A crispy crunchy medley of toasty ingredients

Recipe on page 83

Rapini Donburi
Add a little milk for a richer flavor
Photo on page 80

This donburi is great in early spring when rapini blossoms are in bloom. In Japan, people celebrate the coming of spring by holding parties under blooming cherry trees. Spring is all about flowers. Why not hold your own "spring is here" celebration and serve this festive donburi snack?

Ingredients (Serves 2)
1/2 bunch rapini (*nanohana*. Or sub. broccoli raab)
1 spicy cod roe sack (*mentaiko*)
Pinch salt (for boiling)
A: 1 Tbsp milk
    1 Tbsp mayonnaise
    1 Tbsp sesame oil
    Pinch each salt and sugar
2 small servings steaming hot rice

Instructions
1) Remove root ends of rapini and cook in boiling water with a pinch of salt for about 20 seconds. Drain well and squeeze. Cut in half.
2) Remove membrane of spicy cod roe and place in a bowl. Add mixture A and blend.
3) Serve rice in cups and top first with rapini, then with cod roe.

Kinpira Lotus Root Donburi
Be generous with the sesame
Photo on page 80

Cook the lotus root well before seasoning for a rich flavor. The heartiness and distinct crunch of lotus root melds with sweet and spicy *kinpira* sauce, creating a perfect match for rice.

Ingredients (Serves 2)
7 oz (200 g) lotus root
    (or sub. water chestnuts, sunchokes or jicama)
Vinegar/water solution
1 Tbsp sesame oil
3 Tbsp roasted white sesame seeds
2 red chili peppers, finely chopped
1 Tbsp mirin (sweet cooking wine)
1 Tbsp soy sauce
2 small servings steaming hot rice

Instructions
1) Peel lotus root (or jicama) and slice into 1/5" (5 mm) rounds. Soak in vinegar water for 3 minutes. Drain and pat dry.
2) Add sesame oil to a heated pan and stir-fry lotus root on high heat.
3) When lotus root is lightly browned, add sesame seeds and finely chopped chili peppers, seeds included. Stir-fry briskly. Add mirin and soy sauce and toss to coat.
4) Serve rice in cups and top with above.

Butter Scallop Donburi
Char scallop surface quickly on high heat
Photo on page 81

Butter sautéed scallops on top of a cup of rice look like luscious little steaks. Don't worry about cooking until well done, just focus on charring the surface for a hearty flavor. Butter, soy sauce, scallions—the list of condiments will make your mouth water all the more.

Ingredients (Serves 2)
4 fresh scallops, patted dry
1 Tbsp vegetable oil
Dash each salt and pepper
2 small servings steaming hot rice
1 Tbsp butter
Dash soy sauce
Chopped spring onions
    (or sub. scallions), to taste

Instructions
1) Pour oil into a heated pan and add scallops. Sprinkle with salt and pepper and cook on high heat until surface is browned. Turn over and cook other side.
2) Serve rice in cups and top with scallops. Immediately top with butter, soy sauce, and pepper. Finish with spring onions (or scallions).

Young Sardine Donburi
Toast young sardines until crispy
Photo on page 81

Toasted little fish so crispy they dissolve as you touch them. Add to that the hearty flavor of roasted sesame seeds and roasted seaweed. This roasty toasty treat can't be beat. Great as a beer snack. Use plenty of Japanese *tsukudani* pepper.

Ingredients (Serves 2)
3 Tbsp *jako* (dried baby sardines)
2 Tbsp dried *wakame* seaweed
2 Tbsp roasted black sesame seeds
2 small servings steaming hot rice
Dried green seaweed (*aonori*), to taste
Japanese pepper *tsukudani* (Japanese
    sansho cooked in sweet soy sauce.
    Or sub. pepper powder), to taste

Instructions
1) Spread baby sardines on top of aluminum foil and toast in a toaster oven (or place under broiler) until thoroughly crispy (appx. 2 to 3 minutes). Cook *wakame* in a microwave oven for 1 minute until crunchy. Do not cover with plastic wrap. Mix sardines, *wakame*, and roasted sesame seeds.
2) Serve rice in cups and top with above. Sprinkle with Japanese pepper and dried green seaweed.

Liver Donburi
Grated onion is the key
Photo on page 81

Place a slab of liver coated in rich, thick sauce onto rice. The fragrant aroma of butter and soy sauce will make you crave a second helping.

Ingredients (Serves 2)
7 oz (200 g) beef liver
A: 1 Tbsp grated onion
    Dash grated garlic
    2 Tbsp mirin (sweet cooking wine)
    1 Tbsp butter
    1 Tbsp sake (or cooking wine)
    1 Tbsp soy sauce
    1 to 2 tsp sugar
1 Tbsp vegetable oil
Dash each salt and pepper
2 small servings steaming hot rice
Bunching onion (or sub. green onions
    or leeks), to taste

Instructions
1) Rinse liver thoroughly and pat dry. Cut to a thickness of 1/3 inch (7 mm). Combine mixture A.
2) Add oil to a heated pan and lay out liver slices. Sprinkle with salt and pepper and cook on medium high heat until brown. Turn over. When both sides are thoroughly browned, remove from pan.
3) Add mixture A to pan and turn heat to high. When butter melts, add cooked liver and coat both sides. Serve rice in cups and top with liver and sauce remaining in pan. Garnish with thin slices of onion (or scallions).

Notes
Beef liver is not very pungent, but if odor is a concern, rub liver with juice from grated ginger before rinsing.

Donburi Companions: Side Dishes

Korean-Style Seasoned Cabbage
The flavor of ginger and sesame will keep your chopsticks moving

Ingredients (Serves 2)
1/4 head cabbage
A: Dash grated ginger
   2 Tbsp ground white sesame
   1 Tbsp sesame oil
   2 pinches each salt and sugar

Instructions
1) Cut cabbage into bite-size pieces and cook in lightly salted boiling water for about 8 minutes. Drain in a colander.
2) Place cabbage in a bowl and add mixture A. Toss to coat.

Spicy Shrimp and Soybean Sprouts
Use the soaking liquid from the shrimp for a full flavor

Ingredients (Serves 2)
1 Tbsp dried shrimp
1/2 C soybean sprouts
3 pinches salt
Chili oil, to taste

Instructions
1) Reconstitute shrimp in 2 Tbsp boiling water. Remove root ends of bean sprouts and cook in boiling water with 1 pinch of salt. Drain in a colander.
2) Place sprouts and shrimp in a bowl and season with shrimp soaking liquid, 2 pinches of salt, and chili oil.

The beauty of a donburi is that it's a complete meal in itself. But adding a companion never hurts. These sides get along so well with their buddy donburi that your appetite will say, "The more the merrier!" So whip up these simple dishes as you prepare a donburi.

Stir-fried Dried Daikon
Cook well and use plenty of sesame
Ingredients (Serves 2)
1 oz (30 g) dried shredded daikon radish
1 sheet thin fried tofu (*aburaage*.
   Or sub. 4 oz Tofu Cutlet)
1/2 nub ginger
1 red chili pepper
1 Tbsp sesame oil
1/2 Tbsp each soy sauce and mirin
   (sweet cooking wine)
1 Tbsp roasted black sesame seeds

Instructions
1) Reconstitute dried daikon as directed on the package and rinse under running water. Drain and squeeze out excess water. Slice fried tofu widthwise into 1/5" (5 mm) strips and julienne ginger. Remove stem and seeds from chili pepper.
2) Add sesame oil to a heated pan and sauté ginger and chili pepper on low heat until fragrant. Add daikon and fried tofu and stir-fry on high heat.
3) When ingredients are coated in oil, season with soy sauce and mirin and stir-fry until ingredients are well coated. Add roasted sesame seeds and mix briefly.

Salted *Komatsuna*
The crispiness is irresistible— all you have to do is add hot water
Ingredients (Serves 2)
1/2 bunch *komatsuna* (or sub. mustard greens, spinach or bok choy)
1/2 tsp salt
Sesame oil, to taste
Roasted black sesame seeds, to taste

Instructions
1) Remove root ends of *komatsuna* (or greens) and cut to 2" (5 cm) lengths. Spread out in a vat and pour hot water over *komatsuna*; drain when softened. Place in a bowl, add salt and massage in by hand. Add sesame oil and toss. Cover with plastic wrap and refrigerate for 15 minutes, stirring occasionally.
2) Serve and garnish with roasted sesame.

Spicy Mayonnaise Daikon Salad
Thinly sliced ginger is the key

Ingredients (Serves 2)
2" (5 cm) segment daikon radish
1/2 nub ginger
A: 1 Tbsp mayonnaise
   1/2 Tbsp milk
   1/2 tsp Japanese mustard paste
      (or sub. hot mustard)
   Pinch salt
   Dash sesame oil
Cayenne pepper, to taste

Instructions
1) Peel daikon and cut into 1/8" (3 mm) rounds, then slice rounds into thin strips. Finely chop ginger.
2) Combine mixture A. Add daikon and coat well. Serve and sprinkle with cayenne pepper.

Lightly Pickled Veggies
Vegetable oil adds a mellow richness

Ingredients (Serves 2)
1/8 head cabbage
1/3 carrot stick
1/2 cucumber
A: 1/4 C (50 ml) water
   1 Tbsp vegetable oil
   1/2 Tbsp mirin (sweet cooking wine)
   1 tsp salt
   2 pinches sugar
Seven-spice (or cayenne) powder, to taste

Instructions
1) Chop cabbage into bite-size pieces. Cut carrot diagonally into 1/8" (2 mm) slices, then chop into thin strips. Slice cucumbers into 1/5" (5 mm) rounds.
2) Combine mixture A in a bowl and add vegetables. Mix well by hand. Cover with plastic wrap and refrigerate for at least 15 minutes. Serve and sprinkle with seven-spice (or cayenne) powder, if desired.

Harusame Salad

Spicy Chinese flavor, sweet browned fish cake, tender glass noodles

Ingredients (Serves 2)
1 oz (30 g) glass noodles (*harusame* or *saifun*)
1 tube-shaped fish cake (*chikuwa*)
   (or sub. 3 oz imitation crab legs,
   browned in oil)
1/3 bunch spring onions (or sub. scallions)
A: Dash grated ginger
   1 Tbsp roasted white sesame seeds
   1 Tbsp sesame oil
   1/2 Tbsp each rice vinegar, soy sauce, and
      oyster sauce
   1 tsp Doubanjiang (Chinese chili paste)
   1/2 tsp sugar

Instructions
1) Soften glass noodles according to package directions. Drain well. Cut fish cake (or crab legs) into 1/5" (5 mm) widths. Cut spring onions to 2" (5 cm) lengths.
2) Combine mixture A in a bowl and add glass noodles, fish cake, and onions. Toss well and serve.

Nutty Cheese Salad

Sweet and salty caramel nuts— irresistibly delicious!

Ingredients (Serves 2)
1 3/4 oz to 2 oz (50 to 60 g) cream cheese
5/6 C nuts of your choice (walnuts, cashews,
   almonds, etc.)
3 Tbsp sugar
2 pinches salt

Instructions
1) Cut cream cheese into 2/5" (1 cm) cubes.
2) Roast nuts in a frying pan on medium heat until lightly browned. Add sugar and melt, stirring only when necessary. When sugar melts and turns a light brown caramel color, stir quickly, add salt, and briefly stir again. Move to a tray to cool. Chop into chunks.
3) Mix together cheese and nuts and serve.

Cheesy Arugula Salad

**Mellow cheese and
refreshingly bitter arugula**

Ingredients (Serves 2)

2 1/2 oz (70 g) arugula
1 to 1 1/2 oz (30 to 40 g) cream cheese
A: Dash grated garlic
   1 Tbsp olive oil
   1/2 Tbsp rice vinegar
   Pinch each salt and sugar
   Dash pepper
Pepper, to taste

Instructions

1) Remove root ends of arugula. Cut cream cheese into 2/5" (1 cm) cubes.
2) Combine mixture A in a bowl, add arugula and cream cheese, and toss. Sprinkle with pepper, if desired.

Potato Salad

**Large cubes of potatoes
with a hint of nutmeg**

Ingredients (Serves 2)

2 potatoes
1/2 cucumber
2 slices ham
A: 1 1/2 Tbsp mayonnaise
   1 Tbsp milk
   1 tsp wholegrain mustard
   2 pinches sugar
   Dash each vegetable oil, curry powder, and
     nutmeg
Salt and pepper, to taste

Instructions

1) Peel potatoes and cut into 1 1/5" (3 cm) cubes. Soak in water for 3 minutes. Place in a saucepan and add just enough water to cover. Simmer with lid on until a skewer can be easily poked through potatoes. Drain.
2) Slice cucumbers into thin rounds and ham into 4/5" (2 cm) cubes.
3) Combine mixture A in a bowl, add potatoes, cucumber, and ham, and stir. Adjust flavor with salt and pepper.

Grilled Eggplant
Just pop them in the toaster oven
Ingredients (Serves 2)
2 eggplants (the small, slender Japanese or
    Chinese variety)
Salted water, for soaking
Vegetable oil
Dash grated ginger
Dash soy sauce

Instructions
1) Peel eggplants with a peeler and quarter
   lengthwise. Soak in salt water for 3 minutes,
   then pat dry. Lightly coat aluminum foil with
   vegetable oil and arrange eggplants on top.
   Toast in a toaster oven (or broiler) for 5 to 8
   minutes.
2) When eggplants are tender and lightly
   browned, move to a plate. Garnish with
   grated ginger and sprinkle with soy sauce.

Butter Sautéed *Kabocha*
Soft and crumbly with deliciously crispy edges
Ingredients (Serves 2)
1/8 *kabocha* (aka Japanese pumpkin.
    Or sub. pumpkin or buttercup squash)
1/2 Tbsp vegetable oil
1/2 to 1 Tbsp butter
Dash salt

Instructions
1) Remove stem of *kabocha* (or squash) and
   cut into 1/4" (7 mm) wedges.
2) Add oil to a heated pan. Arrange *kabocha* and
   sprinkle with salt. Cover and cook on medium
   low heat until lightly browned on one side.
   Turn over, cover again and cook other side.
3) When *kabocha* is soft enough for a skewer to
   be poked through, add butter and coat both
   sides. Serve and sprinkle with salt, if desired.

Pickled Daikon Salad

Pickles make the salad

Ingredients (Serves 2)
5 slices pickled daikon (*takuan*),
   1/8" (3 mm) thick
1/4 head lettuce
A: 1 Tbsp sesame oil
   1 Tbsp roasted white sesame seeds
   1/2 Tbsp rice vinegar
   2 pinches sugar
   Pinch salt

Instructions
1) Julienne pickled daikon. Shred lettuce into bite-size pieces.
2) Combine mixture A in a bowl and add pickled daikon and lettuce. Toss well and serve.

Lightly Dressed Tofu

Dried shrimp add heartiness and sesame oil completes the flavor

Ingredients (Serves 2)
1/2 block firm tofu
1/3 bunch spring onions (or scallions)
2 to 3 Tbsp *sakura* shrimp (dried dwarf shrimp.
   Or sub. salad shrimp)
1 Tbsp sesame oil
Pinch sugar
Salt, to taste

Instructions
1) Wrap tofu in a paper towel and place in a colander or sieve. Press using a dish or other heavy object as a weight for about 15 minutes to thoroughly drain excess water. Chop spring onions (or scallions) to 2" (5 cm) lengths.
2) Place tofu in a bowl and break up into chunks with a wooden spatula. Add spring onions, shrimp, sesame oil, and sugar and toss. Adjust flavor with salt.

Sesame-Dressed Chicken Cucumber Salad
Crunchy cucumbers are a delight

Ingredients (Serves 2)
2 chicken breasts
2 cucumbers
Dash salt
A: 1 Tbsp each ground sesame seeds and mayonnaise
   1/2 Tbsp sesame oil
   Pinch salt

Instructions
1) Cook chicken breasts in boiling water with a dash of salt until cooked through. Shred meat. Peel cucumbers with a peeler and julienne.
2) Combine mixture A in a bowl, add chicken and cucumbers, and toss.

Cilantro Salad
This salad will make you fall in love with cilantro!

Ingredients (Serves 2)
1 bunch cilantro
A: Dash grated garlic
   Dash grated ginger
   1 Tbsp each sesame oil and soy sauce
   1/2 Tbsp lemon juice
   1/2 tsp sugar

Instructions
1) Remove root ends and thick stems of cilantro and cut to 1 1/5" (3 cm) lengths.
2) Combine mixture A in a bowl, add cilantro, and toss.

Donburi Companions: Soups

As you munch away at a lip-smackingly delicious donburi, occasionally stop your chopsticks for a sip of soup. What a sublime experience.
Of course you could sip a cup of tea, and that would be satisfying too.
But try a donburi-friendly cup of soup.
You'll think this must be how people eat in heaven.

Chinese-Style Corn Soup

Chinese-Style Corn Soup

The secret seasoning is sesame oil; enjoy the pleasantly sweet and mellow flavor

Ingredients (Serves 2)
8 oz (230 g) canned creamed corn
A: 1/2 Tbsp potato (or corn) starch
   1 Tbsp water
1 2/3 C milk
1/2 bouillon cube
Salt, pepper, and sugar to taste
Dash sesame oil

Instructions
1) Combine mixture A.
2) Pour creamed corn into a saucepan and add milk a little at a time. Add bouillon cube and place over medium heat. Mix constantly with a wooden spoon. When soup starts to boil, season with salt, pepper, and sugar to taste.
3) Turn off heat. Add mixture A after stirring well. Stir soup immediately with wooden spoon. Turn heat back on to medium and simmer until thickened. Finish with sesame oil.

Seaweed Soup

Japanese-style soup with the rich aroma of roasted seaweed

Ingredients (Serves 2)
2 1/2 C water
2" (5 cm) square *konbu* seaweed
Handful dried bonito flakes
A: 1/2 Tbsp mirin (sweet cooking wine)
   1 tsp light soy sauce
Salt, to taste
1 sheet roasted seaweed
Chopped spring onions (or scallions),
   to taste

Instructions
1) Place water and lightly-rinsed *konbu* in a saucepan and let sit for 15 minutes. Place over medium heat. When water starts to boil, remove *konbu* and add bonito flakes. Simmer on low heat for 2 minutes. Scoop out flakes with a sieved ladle and squeeze liquid into sauce pan.
2) Add mixture A. Add salt to taste.
3) Shred roasted seaweed by hand and place in bowls. Pour steaming hot soup over seaweed and sprinkle with spring onions.

Chicken Soup
Enjoy the scent of garlic and pepper

Ingredients (Serves 2)
5 1/4 oz (150 g) chicken thigh
1/2 small bunching onion
   (or sub. green onion or leek)
2 1/2 C boiling water
1 clove garlic
2 to 3 thin slices ginger
1 Tbsp mirin (sweet cooking wine)
1 tsp oyster sauce
Salt and pepper, to taste

Seaweed Soup

Chicken Soup

Spicy Vegetable Soup

Instructions

1) Remove fat from chicken and cut into 2/5" (1 cm) slices. Mince white end of bunching onion (or leek).
2) Bring water to boil in a pan and add chicken, green part of onion, garlic, and ginger. When water comes to boil again, lower heat. Simmer for 10 minutes, occasionally removing bitter foam that floats to the surface.
3) Remove green onion stems, ginger, and garlic. Add mirin and oyster sauce and mix. Adjust flavor with salt and pepper. Serve and sprinkle with minced bunching onion from step 1 and pepper.

Spicy Vegetable Soup
Simmered vegetables enrich the flavor of this luxurious soup

Ingredients (Serves 2)
3 1/2 oz (100 g) boneless pork
   loin, sliced
1/8 head Napa cabbage
1 bunch garlic chives
1 clove garlic
1 nub ginger
1 Tbsp sesame oil
1 Tbsp Doubanjiang
   (Chinese chili paste)
Dash each salt and pepper
2 Tbsp sake (or cooking wine)
2 1/2 C water
1 Tbsp each oyster sauce and
   mirin (sweet cooking wine)
Soy sauce, to taste

Instructions

1) Separate Napa cabbage into stems and leaves. Coarsely chop leaves and thinly slice stems into 2" (5 cm) strips. Cut garlic chives to 2" (5 cm) lengths. Mince garlic and ginger.
2) Pour sesame oil into a heated pan and sauté garlic, ginger and Doubanjiang on low heat until fragrant. Add pork and season with salt and pepper. Stir-fry on high heat.
3) When pork is lightly browned, add stems and leaves of Napa cabbage (in that order) and stir-fry. When vegetables are coated with oil, add sake and stir-fry quickly, then add water, oyster sauce and mirin. Bring to boil and lower heat. Simmer for 5 minutes, occasionally removing bitter foam that floats to the surface. Add garlic chives and simmer briefly. Adjust flavor with soy sauce.

Julienned Vegetable Soup

Savor the simplicity of root vegetables with an accent of pepper

Ingredients (Serves 2)

2" (5 cm) daikon
2" (5 cm) carrot
4" (10 cm) celery
1 clove garlic
1 Tbsp olive oil
2 1/2 C boiling water
1/2 bouillon cube
Salt and pepper, to taste

Instructions

1) Peel daikon, carrot, and celery and slice lengthwise into thin julienne strips. Mince garlic.
2) Put olive oil in a heated pan and sauté garlic on low heat until fragrant. Add carrot, daikon, and celery, in that order. Lightly season with salt and pepper and stir-fry on high heat.
3) When vegetables are coated in oil, add boiling water and bouillon cube. Bring to a boil and cook for 8 minutes, occasionally removing the bitter foam that floats to the surface. Adjust flavor with salt and pepper. Serve and sprinkle with pepper, if desired.

Julienned Vegetable Soup   Home-Style Miso Soup

Home-Style Miso Soup

The soothing essence of Japanese home-style cooking

Ingredients (Serves 2)

1/2 block tofu
2 1/2 C boiling water
Handful dried bonito flakes
2 Tbsp miso
Spring onions (or scallions), to taste

Instructions

1) Cut tofu into bite-size cubes and slice onions (or scallions) into rounds.
2) Bring water to boil in a saucepan and add bonito flakes. Turn heat to low and simmer for 2 minutes. Turn off heat. Scoop out bonito flakes with a sieved ladle and squeeze liquid into saucepan.
3) Add tofu to soup stock and simmer on medium heat. Add miso to taste, dissolving slowly. Serve and sprinkle with onions (or scallions).

Red Miso Soup   Curry Soup with Bacon and Celery

Curry Soup with Bacon and Celery

Enjoy the refreshing flavor of celery

Ingredients (Serves 2)

3 slices bacon
1 stalk celery
1/2 small tomato
1 clove garlic
1 Tbsp + 1 tsp olive oil
1 Tbsp white wine
2 1/2 C water
1/2 bouillon cube
1 tsp curry powder
Salt and pepper, to taste

Instructions

1) Cut bacon into 2/5" (1 cm) pieces. Peel celery and cut stem diagonally into thin slices. Shred celery leaves. Cut tomato into 2/5" (1 cm) cubes. Mince garlic.
2) Put 1 Tbsp olive oil in a heated pan and sauté garlic on low heat until fragrant. Add bacon and sauté on medium heat until coated in oil. Add celery stem and stir-fry on high heat.
3) When celery is slightly tender, add white wine and stir-fry briefly. Add water, bouillon cube and curry powder and simmer. Bring to a boil then lower heat. Simmer 3 to 5 minutes, occasionally removing the bitter foam that floats to the surface.
4) Adjust flavor with salt and pepper, add tomato and celery leaves, and simmer briefly.
5) Serve and add pepper and 1 tsp olive oil, if desired.

Red Miso Soup

Boil briefly after adding miso

Ingredients (Serves 2)

1 sheet thin fried tofu (*aburaage*.
   Or sub. 4 oz Tofu Cutlet)
1/2 pack *enoki* mushrooms
1/2 bunching onion
   (or sub. green onion or leek)
2 1/2 C boiling water
Handful dried bonito flakes
2 Tbsp red miso

Instructions

1) Slice fried tofu to 1/3" (7 mm) widths. Cut off root end of *enoki* mushrooms. Cut bunching onion (or leek) diagonally into 2/5" (1 cm) slices.
2) Bring water to boil in a saucepan and add bonito flakes. Turn heat to low and simmer for 2 minutes. Turn off heat. Scoop out bonito flakes with a sieved ladle and squeeze out liquid.
3) Add ingredients from step 1 and simmer on medium heat. When bunching onion and mushrooms are tender, add miso to taste, dissolving slowly.

Kentaro Kobayashi

Born 1972 in Tokyo, Japan. Began working as an illustrator while attending Musashino Art University. With "easy yet delicious, stylish yet realistic" as his motto, Kentaro began displaying his creativity and outstanding cooking sense in magazines and on television shortly thereafter. As a popular culinary artist representing a younger generation, he proposes delicious yet accessible dishes with energy and flair. The recipe book you hold in your hands is demonstrative of his passion for unleashing the delicious flavor of rice.

Donburi Mania

Translation: Patricia Kawasaki
Vetting: Lisa Reilly

Published by Vertical, Inc., New York.

Originally published in Japanese as *Tobikkirino, Donburi* by Bunka Shuppankyoku, Tokyo, 2002.

ISBN 978-1-934287-49-1

Manufactured in The United States of America

First American Edition

Vertical, Inc.
www.vertical-inc.com